# EDWARD KELLY

### THE ENGLISHMAN'S

# TWO EXCELLENT TREATISES

#### ON THE

# PHILOSOPHER'S STONE,

##### TOGETHER WITH

# THE THEATRE OF TERRESTRIAL ASTRONOMY.

---

WITH EMBLEMATIC FIGURES.

Now first published for the Benefit of the
Sons of Hermes by J. L. M. C.
(that is, John Lilly and Meric Casaubon).

Two Excellent Treatises on the
Philosopher's Stone.

This reprint published 1991 by

The Banton Press
Nelson St, Largs
Scotland.


ISBN: 1 85652 103 6

# CONTENTS.

# BIOGRAPHICAL PREFACE.

----

"I VENTURE to hope," says the subject of this memoir, in his treatise entitled *De Lapide Philosophorum*, "that my life and character will so become known to posterity that I may be counted among those who have suffered much for the sake of truth." The justification thus modestly desired by Edward Kelly has not been accorded him by the supreme court of judgment to which he appealed. Posterity continues to regard him in much the same light as he was looked at by the men of his immediate period, as a fraudulent notary who was deservedly deprived of his ears; as a sordid impostor, who duped the immeasurable credulity of the learned Doctor Dee, and subsequently involved his victim in transactions which have permanently

degraded an otherwise great name ;
finally, as a pretended transmuter of
metals, who was only too leniently treated
by the emperor whom he deceived. For
example, the astrologer depicted by
Hudibras had read

" Dee's prefaces before
The Devil, and Euclid o'er and o'er,
And all th' intrigues 'twixt him and Kelly,
Lexas and th' Emperour would tell ye."

But to Doctor Dee, at least, this
is demonstrably unjust. This is the
verdict of posterity in so far as
it has concerned itself with the subject ;
it is the verdict of the biographical
dictionaries, who have faithfully tran-
scribed from one another, after the
easy method which prevails with biographical dictionaries when they deal
with magicians and seers, with alchemists
and other professors of mystic physics,
as, generally, with all the oracles of the
borderland ; and, in so far as it con-
cerns itself with borderlands, unerudite
public opinion has been led by the
erudite ignorance of the dictionaries.

Now, in offering for the first time to the English reader the three very curious treatises which constitute the chief literary remains of Edward Kelly, it is not necessary, as it would be in fact without reason, that the editor should accept an indiscriminate brief for the defence of the alchemist who wrote them. To the collector of curiosities in science and *choses inouies* in literature, the interest which may attach to them will be unimpaired by the mummeries or crimes of their author. For the student of Hermetic antiquities, it will become evident, and he may already be aware, that the value of the *duo tractatus* and their complement is not that they are the work of an adept, but that they comprehend a careful digest or concensus of alchemical philosophers. while the interest which attaches to the man is created by his possession for a period of the two tinctures of alchemical philosophy, and not in his ability to compose them. At the same time, the adventures and imprisonments of Kelly, with

his transitions from abject poverty to
sudden wealth, from a proscribed and
law hunted fugitive to a baron or
marshal of Bohemia, and then again to
disgrace and imprisonment, ending in
a death of violence, to say nothing of his
visions and transmutations, constitute
an astonishing narrative, and make up
the broad outlines of a life which would
be possible alone in the seventeenth and
eighteenth centuries.  Moreover, here,
as in so many other cases, the student
of transcendental history will hardly
need to be informed that the " skryer "
of Doctor Dee and the discoverer of
the so-called " Book of Saint Dunstan "
has been accredited with many iniquities
of which he does not seem to have been
guilty.

If it be permissible to set aside for
the moment the mere antiquarian interest in these remains of Edward Kelly,
and to exhibit a preferential attention
towards that point of view from which
the Hermetic student would be disposed to regard them, it will be reason-

able to affirm that the importance of
this alchemist's history concentrates
entirely in his possession of the transmuting powders, and in the manner by
which he is said to have acquired them.
The other episodes of his life may be
treated with comparative brevity.

Edward Kelly appears to have been
born at Worcester, the event occurring,
according to Anthony à Wood,* about
four o'clock in the afternoon on the first
day of August, 1555. This was in the
third year of Queen Mary's reign. He
was educated in his native city until the
age of seventeen, when he is supposed
to have repaired to Oxford. The regis-
ters of that University contain no record
of any Edward Kelly having entered at
the period in question, and it is assumed
that his real name was Talbot. Three
persons bearing this designation were
entered at Gloucester Hall about this
time. Possibly the University records
have not been adequately searched, and

---

* *Athenæ Oxoniensis*, ed. 1813, pp. 639-643.

if not, the evidence for his sojourn at Oxford is of a very slender character.*
If, beyond the difficulty that has been mentioned, there are no other reasons for supposing that he changed his name, and none others seem forthcoming, there is, perhaps, more reason to discredit his university career than to accept the theory of the *alias*. If he were at Oxford, it would be only for a short period, and he is said to have left abruptly. Other narratives state that he was bred as an apothecary, and in this way acquired some skill in chemistry. It was more probably the profession of his father, of which he may have picked up some knowledge in boyhood. After the termination of his scholastic studies, whether at Oxford or elsewhere, he himself seems to have embraced the law, and to have settled in London, or, according to another account, at Lancaster, but possibly in both places. It

---

* The amanuensis of Thomas Allen (*temp.* Wood), of Gloucester Hall, said that Kelly spent some time in that house.

was in the latter certainly that his troubles began. He was a skilful penman, who had been at the pains to acquaint himself with archaic English, and, as a Worcester man, not improbably with Welsh, and by the help of these accomplishments he was accused of producing forged title deeds in the interests of a client. The indictment is very vague, and does not rest upon anything which can be termed evidence. He is said, however, but upon equally uncertain grounds, to have been pilloried at Lancaster, and to have been also deprived of his ears. There is no doubt that he fell into grievous trouble, for to his life's end he was always less or more in fear of English law, and sometimes seems to have preferred a foreign prison to the uncertain reception which was to be anticipated on his return home. But that the penalty which his biographers have meted out to him, whether deserved or not by his misdeeds, was in some way evaded, it seems more reasonable to think. The

distinguished position which he held
subsequently at the Court of the Emperor Rodolph, would have scarcely been
possible to a man who had lost his
ears. The credulity of royal person-
ages at the end of the seventeenth
century may have facilitated many im-
postures on the part of the alchemists
whom they protected, but could scarcely
have extended to accepting the philosophical illumination of an adept who
had been branded by law. The alterna-
tive story is, then, apparently preferable,
and this says that Kelly sought refuge
in Wales. Here it is exceedingly prob-
able that he adopted an assumed name,
but whether Talbot became Kelly or
whether Kelly merged for a moment
into Talbot, or some other designation,
is a mystery of modification in Alchemy
which the past is not likely to give up
In Wales he would seem to have embraced a nomadic life, staying at
obscure inns, and after a time he must
have worked his way down into the
neighbourhood of the historic abbey of

Glastonbury.* What occurred to him here, what was destined, in fact, to be the turning point in the life of this fugitive, has been recited by more than one of his biographers; and if, in the present narrative, it be based on the record of the French scientific *littéra-teur*, Louis Figuier, that is not because his account is specially preferable, but because it is nearest at the moment.†

He put up, among other places, at a lonely hostelry in the mountains, and there it came to pass that he was shewn an old manuscript which no one in the village could decipher. Kelly had good, if somewhat mournful reason to be well acquainted with the mysteries of ancient writing,‡ and he saw at a glance not only that it was in the old Welsh language,§ but

---

* It is about 35 miles from Glastonbury to the nearest part of South Wales.

† *L'Alchimie et les Alchimistes.* Troisième édition Paris, *1860*, p. 232, *et seq.*

‡ The insinuation is that Edward Kelly, as above indicated, had been concerned in the fraudulent manufacture of ancient legal documents.

§ Outside M. Figuier's imagination there does not seem to be any reason for supposing that the manuscript was in Welsh.

that it treated of the transmutation of metals. He made inquiries as to the history of this bibliographical rarity, and learned that its discovery was due to one of those outbursts of religious fanaticism which were common enough in the reign of Queen Elizabeth. The sepulchre of a departed bishop interred in a neighbouring church had been violated, the zeal of the Protestant being not unmixed with the desire of obtaining hidden treasures. However, the sacrilegious act was only rewarded by the alchemical manuscript which the despoilers could not read, and by two small ivory caskets, containing respectively a red and a white powder, which in their eyes were equally useless. The receptacle of the red powder was shattered in their fury, and much of its contents were lost. What remained of it, together with the second casket and the accompanying document, they readily disposed of to the innkeeper, who seems to have had a hand in the discreditable transaction, in exchange for a flagon of wine. The manuscript was retained as a curiosity to be exhibited to strangers frequenting the hostelry ; the intact casket was a plaything for the innkeeper's children ; the remnant of the red powder seems to have remained by chance in its shattered receptacle ; and it came to pass, in due time, that Kelly, in his capacity as a stranger, examined the entire treasure-trove. If Kelly had begun life as an apothecary, he had doubtless a smattering of chemistry, * and there would have been few educated persons at that period who, in connection with Alchemy, had heard nothing of the red and white tinctures which were the instruments of the *Magnum Opus.* He knew enough to be anxious to possess them, and for the whole archaic collection he offered one guinea to the innkeeper, who accepted these terms.

---

\* Figuier observes that he was devoid of the most elementary conception of chemistry or of transmutatory philosophy, but then Figuier was a Frenchman and drew largely upon those interior resources which economise documentary research.

Such is the narrative of the discovery, stripped of a few elaborations, which are due to Gallic insight. Now, Nash,* who is responsible for the story of the pillory, assigns no date for the supposed mutilation of Edward Kelly, but it may be regarded as having taken place, if at all, about 1580. If the mutilation in question be rejected, the same date will serve us as the commencement of the Welsh wanderings. After he had secured the Hermetic treasures his occupations for a time are uncertain; when he reappears it is in company with Dr. John Dee. Figuier, still elaborating upon the outlines of unfanciful and ineffective biographers, recounts how, being unable to make use of his treasures, through his alleged ignorance of chemistry, he had recourse to his old friend Dee, wrote to him on the subject, received a favourable reply, and forthwith betook himself to London. Whether he wrote or not, there he was

---

* History and Antiquities of Worcester, 2 vols., London, 1781, etc., Fol.

evidently established in the autumn of
1582. It is difficult to decide whether
this was a first acquaintance. Lenglet
du Fresnoy, who was fairly careful in
the collection of his data, states that
Kelly was really a notary of London,
and that Dee was his old neighbour and
friend.* They are supposed to have
set to work together, and in the month
of December, 1579, it is said, in the

---

* There is a very large mass of material in existence for
the life of Dr. Dee, and it has been so imperfectly investi-
gated that the biography of this singular man is still practically unwritten. So far as it has been possible to examine
it for the purposes of this notice, it does not seem to afford
much assistance on this debatable point. The Autobiographical Tracts of Dr. John Dee, Warden of the College of
Manchester, edited by Mr. James Crossley, were printed for
the Chetham Society in 1851, but they do not contain a
single reference to Edward Kelly, nor to any experiments in
Alchemy. In repudiating the magical practices which were
ascribed to him, he refers to certain "false information
given in by one George Ferrys and Prideaux, that I endea-
voured by enchantments to destroy Queene Mary," for which
he was imprisoned at Hampton Court, "even in the weeke
next before the same Whitsuntide that her Majesty (*i.e.*, Queen
Elizabeth, before her accession) was there prisoner also."
There is also a tract occasioned by the accusation that he was
"a conjuror, a caller of devils, a great doer therein, and so
(as some would say) the arche conjuror of this whole kingdom." Concerning which, he says that it is "a damnable

laboratory of a goldsmith, they accomplished a transmutation of metals which
proved the richness of Kelly's tincture
to be one upon two hundred and
seventy-two thousand two hundred and
thirty; but, it is added, "they lost
much gold in experiments before they
knew the extent of its power." If this
date can be accepted, Kelly was then
twenty-four years old, and his companion was his senior by something like

---

slander, utterly untrue, in the whole, and in every worde
and part thereof : as (before the King of Kings) will appere
at the dreadfull day." But, as Halliwell justly remarks,
the "Compendious Rehearsall" was "written for an especial
purpose, for the perusal of royal commissioners, and he has,
of course, carefully avoided every allusion which could be
construed in an unfavourable light. In the other, however
(*i.e.*, in the 'Private Diary'), he tells us of his dreams,
talks of mysterious noises in his chamber, evil spirits, and
alludes to various secrets of occult philosophy in the spirit of
a true believer." The "Private Diary of Dr. John Dee,
and the Catalogue of his Library of Manuscripts," was
edited by James Orchard Halliwell, F.R.S., for the Cam-
den Society, in 1842. The name of Talbot is mentioned,
*s.v.*, March 9th, 1582, and recurs once or twice further on,
but there seems no reason for identifying it with that of
Edward Kelly, whose initials are not found till November
22nd, 1582, when there is the following brief note :—
"E. K. went to London, and so the next day conveied by
road toward Blakley, and within ten days to return."

thirty years. But the dates are not easy to reconcile at this period, and the diaries of Dr. Dee make no mention of the subject till several years have elapsed.* There is naturally no reason to doubt that they soon made experiments with the powders, and as the *bona fides* of Dr. Dee cannot be seriously challenged through any of the subsequent transactions, he must have regarded the results as satisfactory; it is, further, evident from his own memoranda, made for his personal use, and not designed for publication, that he was not only convinced of the actuality of Kelly's transmutations, but that he had formed a high estimate of his companion's proficiency in Alchemy, and seems always to have received his communications on this subject with gratitude and reverence.† But it would

---

* After September 21st, 1583, there is a gap in the "Private Diary," which is resumed in July, 1586, and presently relates a transmutation performed by Kelly during their sojourn abroad.

† "May 10, 1588. E. K. did open the great secret to me, God be thanked." Again: "Aug. 24, 1580. *Vidi*

appear also that, both in England during the period in question, and afterwards abroad, Dr. Dee was far more profoundly and lastingly interested in the mysteries of visions in the crystal than in the accomplishment of the metallic *magnum opus.* His references to Alchemy are few and far between, but his communications with angels and planetary spirits, and indifferently with all sorts and conditions of invisible intelligences, were recorded in writing by himself with the most scrupulous and exhaustive fidelity. They were subsequently deciphered, arranged, and published in a large folio volume ; and constitute to this day not only the most prolific source of information as to the relations between himself and Kelly, but, in spite of all modern marvels, remain the most curious account extant in the English language of alleged intercourse with the world of spirits. And,

---

*divinam aquam demonstratione magnifici nomini et amici mei incomparabilis, D. Ed. Kellæi ante meridiem tertia hora."* Once more : "Dec. 14. Mr. Edward Kelly gave me the water, earth, and all."

whatever has been advanced to the contrary by sensational biographers like
Louis Figuier, elaborating with a view
to effect, it was not in the main as an
alchemist, but as a seer in the crystal
that Edward Kelly posed before the
doctor of Mortlake. It was also in that
capacity that he chiefly influenced his
companion. It is immaterial for the
purposes of this notice, which, as already
intimated, is not devised as an apology
for its subject, to determine whether
the visions of Edward Kelly were
genuine or not. In the present state of
psychological knowledge, imperfect as
it still is, it is, on the one hand, too
late to deny that a state of lucidity can
be frequently induced by the mediation
of crystals and similar transparent substances ; while it is evident, on the
other hand, from the history of the
subject, that beyond the bare fact and
such possibilities as may be reasonably
attached to it, nothing of real moment
has resulted from any such experiments.
Edward Kelly may have lost his ears

for forgery, or he may have deserved
to be deprived of them, and he may
still have been a genuine clairvoyant,
for the faculty does not suppose an
advanced, or even tolerable, morality
in its possessor. He may equally have
been guiltless of any otherwise illegal
practices, and still he may have shame-
fully imposed upon his friend. There
is only one fact of importance for this
notice—that Edward Kelly, apparently
by no desert of his own, came into
possession of the two tinctures of Hermetic philosophy. Convict or martyr,
seer or cheating conjuror, knave or saint,
matters nothing in comparison. He
may further have accounted for his possession of the tinctures by a romantic
fiction, but this in itself is trivial. At
the same time, with regard to his
visions, it must be admitted that either
he was a clairvoyant of advanced grade,
or he was a man of most ingenious in-
vention.* Between the period of his

---

\* Disraeli, in his "Amenities of Literature," observes
that "the masquerade of his spiritual beings was most re-
markable for its fanciful minuteness."

alleged departure from Oxford and the completion of his twenty-fifth year, he has been accused of so many crimes, not one of which could have been effected without a considerable apprenticeship, that, assuming an extraordinary capacity for misdeeds, it is really somewhat difficult to believe that he could have accomplished so much in so short a space of time. The list includes necromancy, dealing with the devil, forgery (as already seen), and the uttering of base coin.*

---

* In June, 1583, an attachment was issued against him for coining, of which his companion declared him guiltless. Whether this was a consequence of some of his miscarrying experiments in Alchemy does not appear, but, in either case, the charge would appear to have been unfounded, or it was not pressed, for he does not seem to have suffered any subsequent inconvenience by reason of it. The accusation of necromancy may have had some foundation, and in this case, whatever moral odium can attach to him on the subject, it goes some way towards proving that in occult matters he acted in good faith, and believed there was some efficacy in those magical processes of which crystallomancy was a part. The original source of the accusation appears to be John Weever's "Discourse of Ancient Funereal Monuments," London, 1631, fol., pp. 45, 46, and is to this effect, that he caused by his incantations a poor man that had been buried in the yard belonging to Law Church, near to Wotton-in-the-Dale, to be taken out of his grave (meaning not the exhumation of

On the 21st of September, 1583, Edward Kelly and his patron left England for the continent. Various reasons have been assigned for this removal, as, for example, that Kelly went in continual fear of his liberty and even his life; that they could not carry on their

---

the body but the evocation of the spirit of the deceased), and to answer to such questions that he then proposed to him." An original letter to Wood signed "Anonymous Philomusus," and preserved among the Tanner MSS. in the Bodleian Library, says that Weever's authority was an accomplice of Kelly at the time of this transaction. As all species of magic were then vulgarly regarded as of Satanic origin, it is obvious, of course, that, from this standpoint, Kelly had commerce with evil spirits. In this connection there is one interesting citation from the "Diary of Doctor Dee." "April 13, 1584, *circa*, 3 *horam*. After a short request made by me to Christ for wisdom and verity to be ministered by Nalvage (*i.e.*, one of the spirits of the crystal), he appeared and spake much to E. K., which he expressed not to me, but at length confessed that he gave him brotherly counsel to leave dealing as an idolater or fornicator against God, by asking counsel of such as he did." Thereupon "E.K. confessed that he had been dealing with the devil." In whatever sense this admission must be understood, the kind of calumnies which it has occasioned may be understood by a passage in "Sibley's Illustration of the Occult Sciences," the work of a profound believer in astrology and magic.

"Edward Kelly was also a famous magician, and the companion and the associate of Dr. Dee, in most of his magical explorations and exploits: having been brought

alchemical experiments under the best circumstances in their own country; that such operations were calculated to make them notorious, and liable to the super-stitious fury of the populace; that Doctor Dee, in particular, had been disappointed of reasonably expected preferment. All

---

into unison with him (as the Doctor himself declares in the preface to his work on the ministration of spirits) by media-tion of the angel Uriel. But Doctor Dee was undoubtedly deceived in his opinion that the spirits which ministered to him were executing the Divine will, and were the messengers and servants of the Deity. Throughout his writings on this subject, he evidently considers them in this light ; which is still more indisputably confirmed by the piety and devotion he invariably observed at all times when these spirits had intercourse with him. And further, when he found his coad-jutor Kelly was degenerating into the lowest and worst species of the magic art, for the purposes of fraud and avaricious gain, he broke off all manner of connection with him, and would never be seen in his company. But it is believed the doctor, a little before his death, became sensible that he had been imposed upon by these invisible agents, and that all their pretence of acting under the auspices of the angel Uriel, and for the honour and glory of God, was but mere hypocrisy and the delusion of the devil. Kelly, being thus rejected and discountenanced by the Doctor, betook himself to the most mean and vile practices of the magic art ; in all of which pursuits money and the works of the devil appear to have been his chief aim. Many wicked and abominable transactions are recorded of him, which were performed by witchcraft and the mediation of infernal spirits; but nothing more *apropos* to the present subof these causes may have contributed to make their departure desirable, and they may not have been actuated by any of them. As to Dee, he enjoyed a considerable share of Court favour, that of royalty included, and there is no reason to suppose that his journey was in search of preferment, or that he contemplated

ject, than what is mentioned by Weaver in his 'Funeral Monuments.' He there records that Kelly, the Magician, with one Paul Waring, who acted as companion and associate in all his conjurations, went together to the church-yard of Walton Ledale, in the country of Lancaster, where they had information of a person being interred, who was supposed to have hidden or buried a considerable sum of money, and to have died without disclosing to any person where it was deposited. They entered the church-yard at exactly twelve o'clock at night; and having had the grave pointed out to them the preceding day, they exorcised the spirit of the deceased by magical spells and incantations, till it appeared before them, and not only satisfied their wicked desires and iniquities, but delivered several strange predictions concerning persons in that neighbourhood, which were literally and exactly fulfilled. It was vulgarly reported of Kelly, that he outlived the time of his compact with the devil, and was seized at midnight by some infernal spirits, who carried him off in the sight of his own wife and children, at the instant he was meditating a mischievous scheme against the minister of his parish, with whom he was greatly at enmity."—This account is simply a tissue of falsehoods, not only as regards the relations of Dee and Kelly, but the place and manner of the alchemist's death. Moreover, Kelly does not appear to have had any issue.

a protracted absence, for he left his
library behind him in his cottage at
Mortlake His wife and his children
accompanied him, as well as the family
of Kelly, who also appears to have been
married, though at what period is un-
known. This considerable party was
completed by Lord Albert Alasko, a
Polish noble, who had sought and obtained the familiar acquaintance of
Doctor Dee during a residence of a
considerable duration in England.*
Whether he was interested in the alche-

---

\* In the "Private Diary," under date of May 1st,
there is the following entry:—*Albertus Laski, Polonus,
Palatinus Scradensis, venit Londinem.* Compare MS.
Donce 363, fol. 125. "The year of our Lord God, 1583,
the last day of April, the Duke or Prince of Vascos, in
Polonia, came to London, and was lodged at Winchester
House." It was at half-past seven in the evening of May
13th, that Dee made his acquaintance. He became a frequent and even continual visitor. The "Autobiographical
Tracts" published by the Chetham Society contain the
following reference:—"Her Majesty (*An.* 1583, *Julii
ultimo*) being informed by the right honourable Earle of
Leicester, that whereas the same day in the morning he had
told me that his honour and the Lord Laski would dine with
me within two daies after, I confessed sincerely unto him,
that I was not able to prepare them a convenient dinner,
unless I should presently sell some of my plate or some of
my pewter for it, etc."

mical experiments of the two Hermetic
confederates does not appear from the
evidence, though it may be reasonably
assumed. But, like Dee himself, he was
profoundly impressed by the spiritual
revelations in the crystal, and the
records exhibit him as a regular and
active participator in the clairvoyant
séances. The entire journey would seem
to have been undertaken at the instance
of Lord Albert Alasko, who had invited
them to visit him at his castle in the
neighbourhood of Cracovia. Hostile
biographers like Figuier have therefore
represented him as the dupe of the two
colleagues, whom they plundered without mercy, with whom they outstayed
their welcome, and were at last shaken
off, not without great difficulty, when
their victim could tolerate them no
longer, and when he was practically
ruined by their rapacity. For all this
there is not a particle of evidence. It
is certain that they did not reach
Cracovia till March 13th, 1584. They
had scarcely arrived in the north of

Germany before Doctor Dee had in-
telligence of the destruction of his
library at Mortlake, by the fury of a
fanatical mob, who took advantage of
the wizard's absence to revenge themselves on his effects. The sequestration
of his rents and his property seems to
have followed quickly on this act of
vandalism. During this period, as
already seen, there is a gap in the
" Private Diary," and it is only imperfectly supplied by the " True and Faithful Relation," which is devoted to the
visions in the crystal. There is no
record of the circumstances under which
they parted from the Polish noble, but
the date of their departure from Cracovia is fixed by the "Faithful Relation"
as the first day of August, 1584, new
style. There is evidence to shew that,
in common with Doctor Dee, he had experienced much from the unreasoning
violence of Edward Kelly's temper ;
but there is no evidence that they parted
unpleasantly. The visions and revelations in the crystal continued abroad as

at home with the utmost regularity and persistence, doing credit as before either to the marvellous clairvoyance of the seer, or to the variety of his imaginative resources, but destined ere long to be stained with one foul record. It is certain, on the other hand, that during this period the alchemical experiments which have been assumed to be the object of their journey do not appear to have been prosecuted. It is even affirmed that, in spite the *Donum Dei*, the two families were sometimes in great poverty. But at length they repaired to Prague, reaching that city seven days after their departure from Cracovia. There all men talked of Alchemy, numbers practised it, half the world credited the marvels concerning it, and supposed processes were more numerous than even the adepts themselves. Inevitably, the possessor of the Bishop's powder, obtained at the digging in Wales, must have been calculated to shine in this city of hierophants, and Edward Kelly came

among them like that artist Elias fore-
told years previously by Paracelsus, and
still expected by his disciples. Within
a very short time all Prague was in
transport, for the adept Kelly was transmuting everywhere, as, for example, at
the house of Thaddæus de Hazek, the
imperial physician, and even initiating
disciples like Nicholas Barnaud and the
Marshal of Rosenberg in the process, if
not in the secret. Many authorities,
including the great name of Gassendus,
have been cited in support of these pro-
digal transmutations, but some who have
been quoted either utter an uncertain
note or are altogether silent. * However
this may be, the whole party became
exceedingly and suddenly affluent, great
in their extravagance, and magnificent
in their retinues. They were invited to

---

* The only discoverable testimony of Gassendus is contained in *De Rebus Terrenis Inanimis*, Lib. III., c. VI.,
*Lugduni Batavorum*, fol. 1658, vol. 2, p. 143. "Deinde
manifesta sunt genera varia imposturarum, quibus versutio-
res fumivenduli illudere solent non modo simplicioribus, sed
nonnullis etiam ex iis, qui se putant oculatories (he has
already spoken of the credulity of believers, more especially
with regard to the forgeries of alchemical literature), dum

the Court of the Emperor Rodolph II.,
King of Hungary and Bohemia, and
they repaired thither, Kelly to dazzle
that potentate by his transmutations,
and to be made a marshal in consequence. Doctor Dee, who knew nothing
of Alchemy, remained in comparative
retirement, while his companion multiplied his extravagances and the enemies
of his sudden success. As time went on,
the philosopher and the alchemist became mutually intolerable, and there was
a distinct rupture between them, the explanation of which must be sought in the
profligacy of the younger man. In April,
1587, while they were at Trobona, a
naked woman, in an apparition described
by Kelly, directed the ' Skryer ' and his
master to use " their two wives in common." Kelly convinced Dee of the *bona*

---

nempe non satis attendunt ad conditionem aut operantis,
aut manus opus peragentis, etc., etc." Such is the preface
to the reference :—" obque asservatam, ut memorant, Pragæ
intra Thaddæi Haggicii ædeis Mercurii libram in aurum con-
versam, infusa a Kelleio Anglo unicâ liquoris rubicun-
dissimâ guttulâ, cujus adhus vestigium sit, qua parte facta
fuit infusio." This is hardly a testimony of Gassendus.

*fides* of the spirit, and after some hesita-
tion, a solemn covenant was drawn up
in accordance with the direction between Doctor Dee, Kelly, Jane Dee,
and Joan Kelly, " as the third part of
the ' Faithful Relation ' testifies."

Meanwhile the powder, diminished
by excessive projection, became exhausted ; it was squandered still further
in futile attempts to increase it ; and
when the Emperor commanded his guest
to produce it in a becoming quantity,
all experiments proved failures. Yet
Kelly had boasted that he was an adept;
he had everywhere paraded his powers ;
he was not the mere heir of the Stone
—he was an illuminated and proficient
master. The Emperor believed all this,
and he believed it even to the end; the
impotence of the exhausted alchemist
was attributed to obstinacy, and the
guest was changed into a prisoner. He
is said to have been confined in a dun-
geon of the castle of Zobeslau. To
regain his liberty he promised to manufacture the Stone, on condition that he

returned to Prague and took counsel
with Dr. Dee. To that city he was
consequently permitted to go back, but
his house was guarded, and as fresh
experiments in the composition of a
transmuting powder were abortive as
ever, the alchemist, seized with rage,
made a futile attempt to escape, which
ended in the murder of one of his
guards.

A second imprisonment, this time
in the castle of Zerner, followed his
violence. Doctor Dee returned alone
to England, but at a date which con-
flicts with many alleged incidents in
the life of his seer. The two confederates seem to have parted amicably, and
they corresponded after their separation.* At the instance of the philosopher
of Mortlake, Queen Elizabeth claimed
the alchemist as her subject, but the

---

\* There seems little doubt that Dr. Dee held the
memory of Kelly in something like affection. Long after
his return to England, under date March 18, 1595, there is
this entry in one of his diaries : " Mr. Francis Garland came
this morning to visit me, and had much talk with me of Sir
Edward Kelly."

Emperor excused himself from releasing him on the ground of the homicide. The second imprisonment of Kelly, according to accepted dates, lasted till the year 1597, when he attempted to escape by a rope, but, falling from a considerable height, sustained such injuries as resulted in his death at the age of forty-two.* His treatise on the "Stone of the Philosophers" was the product of his enforced leisure, but it did not appease his captor. The other tracts contained in the present volume may have been earlier compositions. As previous to his acquaintance with Kelly Dr. Dee had no transactions in Alchemy, so, after his return to England till his own death in the year 1608, he eschewed experiments which had involved his clairvoyant in misery, and

---

* "John Weever says that Queen Elizabeth sent, very secretly, Captain Peter Gwinne, with some others, to persuade Kelly to return to his native country. It is then said that attempting to escape from a wall of his own house at Prague, he fell, etc. . . . His house is said to bear his name to this day, and was once an old sanctuary."—*Athenæ Oxoniensis.*

was content to be Warden of Manchester, to be persecuted by the Fellows
of the College, and to suffer other in-
dignities with the patience of an en-
lightened philosopher.

---

## II.

### The Book of St. Dunstan.

The student of alchemical literature will naturally be curious to know
whether the mysterious manuscript of
Glastonbury has been pretended to have
survived.  Tradition has ascribed to it
the name which heads this section, and
there is the following evidence, which
must be taken with all faults, to account
for it.  The abbey of Glastonbury was
founded by Saint Dunstan, but he does
not appear to have been buried there,
despite the supposed translation of
his relics from Canterbury.  Yet it
must be inferred from the tradition
that the remains of the disinterred
bishop were those of the saint himself.  Saint Dunstan was supposed to

have been an alchemist, and has been regarded as the patron of the goldsmiths; but an anonymous compiler in manuscript of the seventeenth century affirms that he " had no other elixir or Philosopher's Stone than the gold and silver which, by the benefit of fishing, was obtained, whereby the kingdom's plate and bullion was procured. For the advancement of the fishing trade, he did advise that three fish days be kept in every week, which caused also more abstinence, and hence the proverb that St. Dunstan took the devil by the nose by his pincers." The " Book of St. Dunstan " is mentioned occasionally in the diaries of Dr. Dee, in connection with the "powder found at the digging in England," and in such a way as to make it a reasonable inference that this name was borne by the Glastonbury manuscript. A work of the same title is the subject of continual reference by the son of the philosopher of Mortlake, Arthur Dee, especially in his *Fasciculus Chemicus*. The British Museum contains

a Latin copy in manuscript of another
treatise by the same author, under the
title of *Arca Arcanorum*, which is followed by the *Tractatus Maximi Domini
Dunstani, Episcopi Cantuariensis, veri
philosophi, de Lapide Philosophico.* Several extant manuscripts, both in Latin
and English, widely at variance in their
dates and in the nature of their contents,
are, however, attributed to St. Dunstan.
The first impression printed at Cassel in
1649. A few ignorant critics have gone
so far as to regard Kelly's own treatise
as the genuine Glastonbury manuscript.
Others, discountenancing the connection
with the saint, have been inclined to
consider two metrical treatises, which
are included by Elias Ashmole in the
*Theatrum Chemicum Britannicum,* as
constituting the original work, though
not, of course, in the original form or
language. There may be little evidence
in support of this hypothesis, but it does
not exceed possibility ; if rejected, the
verses in question may be safely regarded as additional literary remains of

Edward Kelly; in either case, they demand a place here.

---

## SIR EDWARD KELLE'S WORK.

All you that faine philosophers would be,
  And night and day in Geber's kitchen broyle,
Wasting the chipps of ancient Hermes' Tree,
  Weening to turn them to a precious oyle,
  The more you worke the more you loose and
    spoile ;
To you, I say, how learned soever you be,
Go burne your Bookes and come and learne of
  me.

Although to my one Booke you have red tenn,
  That's not enough, for I have heard it said
The greatest clarkes are not the wisest men :
  A lion once a silly mouse obey'd.
  In my good will so hold yourselves appaid,
And though I write not halfe so sweete as
    Tully,
Yet shall you finde I trace the stepps of Lully.

Yt doth you good to thinke how your desire
  And self-conceit doth warrantize vaine hope ;
You spare no cost, you want no coals for fier,
  You know the vertues of the Elitrope ;
  You thinke yourselves farr richer than the
    pope ;
What thinge hath being either high or low
But their *materia prima* you do know.

Elixir vitæ and the precious Stone
   You know as well as how to make an apple ;
If 'te come to the workinge then let you alone
   You know the coullers black, brown, bay,
      and dapple ;
   Controwle you once then you begin to fraple,
Swearing and saying, what a fellow is this ?
Yet still you worke, but ever worke amisse.

No, no, my friends, it is not vauntinge words,
   Nor mighty oaths that gaines that sacred
      skill ;
It is obteined by grace and not by swords,
   Nor by greate reading, nor by long sitting still,
   Nor fond conceit, nor working all by will,
But, as I said, by grace it is obteined ;
Seek grace therefore, let folly be refrained.

It is no costly thing I you assure
   That doth beget Magnesia in hir kind ;
Yet is hir selfe by leprosie made pure,
   Hir eyes be cleerer being first made blind,
   And he that can earth's fastnes first unbind
Shall quickly know that I the truth have tould
Of sweete Magnesia, wife to purest gold.

Now what is meant by man and wife is this,
   Agent and patient, yet not two but one,
Even as was Eva Adam's wife I wisse,
   Flesh of his flesh and bone of his bone—
   Such is the unionhood of our precious Stone ;
As Adam slept untill his wife was made,
Even so our Stone ; there can no more be said.

By this you se how thus it came to pass
　　That first was man, and woman then of him ;
Thus Adam here as first and cheefest was,
　　And still remained a man of perfect limme ;
　　Then man and wife were joyned together
　　　　trimme,
And each in love to other straight addressed
　　them,
And did increase their kind when God had
　　blessed them.

Even so the man our Stone is laid to sleepe,
　　Until such time his wife be fully wrought ;
Then he awakes, and joyfully doth keep
　　His new made spouse which he so dearely
　　　　bought ;
　　And when to such perfection they be brought,
Rejoyce the beauty of so fair a bride,
Whose worth is more than halfe the world
　　beside.

I doubte as yet you hardly understand
　　What man or wife doth truly signifie,
And yet I know you beare your selves in hand
　　That out of doubt it Sulpher is and Mercury ;
　　And so it is, but not the common certeinly ;
But Mercury essentiall is trewly the trew wife
That kills her selfe to bring her child to life.

For first and formest she receives the man,
　　Her perfect love doth make her soone con-
　　　　ceive,
Then doth she strive with all the force she can,

In spite of love, of life him to bereave,
  Which being done, then will she never leave,
But labour kindly like a loving wife
Untill againe she him have brought to life.

Then he againe, her kindness to requite,
  Upon her head doth set a crowne of glory,
And to her praise he poems doth indite,
    Whose poems make each poet write a story,
    And that she slew him then she is not sorry,
For he by vertue of his loving wife
Not only lives but also giveth life.

But here I wish you rightly understand
  How here he makes his concubine his wife,
Which if you know not, do not take in hand
    This worke, which unto fooles is nothing rife,
    And look you make attonement where is
        strife ;
Then strip the man into his shirt of tishew,
And her out of her smock to ingender yssue.

To tell you troath he wanteth for no wives,
  In land or sea, in water, air, or fire,
Without their deaths he waieth not their lives.
    Except they live he wants his chief desire ;
    He binds them prentice to the rightest dier,
And when they once all sorrowes have abidden,
Then find they joyes which from them first
        were hidden.

For then they finde the joy of sweet encrease ;
  They bring forth children beautifull to sight,

The which are able prisners to release,
  And to the darkest bodyes give true light,
  Their heavenly tincture is of such great
    might ;
Oh ! he that can but light on such a treasure,
Who would not think his joyes were out of
    measure ?

Now by this question I shall quickly know
  If you can tell which is his wife indeede—
Is she quick footed, fair faced, yea or no ?
  Flying or fixed, as you in bookes do reade ?
  Is she to be fed or else doth she feed ?
Wherein doth she joy, where's her habitation ?
Heavenly or earthly, or of a strange nation ?

What is she, poore ? or is she of any wealth ?
  Bravely of her attyre, or meane in her
    apparrell ?
Or is she sick ? or is she in perfect health ?
  Mild of her nature ? or is she given to
    quarrell ғ
  Is she a glutton ? or loves she the barrell ?
If any one of these you name her for to be,
You know not his wife, nor ever did her see.

And that will I prove to you by good reason,
  That truly noe one of all these is she ;
This is a question to you that is geason ;
  And yet some parte of them all she must be :
  Why then, some parte is not all you may see.
Therefore the true wife which I doe mean
Of all these contraries is the meane betweene.

As meale and water joyned both together
  Is neither meale nor water now but dow,
Which being baked is dow nor water neither :
  Nor any more will each from other goe ;
  The meane betweene is wife, our wife, even so,
And in this hidden point our seacret lyes—
It is enough, few words content the wise.

Now by this simile heere I do reveale
  A mighty seacret, if you marke it well ;
Call mercury water, imagine sulphur meale,
  What meale I meane I hope the wise can tell ;
  Bake them by craft, make them together
    dwell,
And in your working make not too much hast,
For wife is not the while she is in paste.

This lesson learn'd, now give me leave to play,
  I shall the fitter be to learne another,
My mind is turn'd cleane cam another way ;
  I do not love sweete secret thoughts to
    smother —
  It is a child you know that makes a mother,
Sith so it is then we must have a childe,
Or else of motherhood we are beguil'd.

What will you say if I a wonder tell you,
  And prove the mother is child and mother
    too ?
Do you not thinke I goe about to sell you
  A bargaine in sport as some are wont to do ?
  Is't possible the mother to weare her infant's
    shoe ?

In faith it is in our philosophy,
As I will prove by reason by and by.

Ripley doth bid you take it for no scorne
   With patience to attend the true conjunction,
For, saith he, in the aire our child is born,
   There he receiveth the holy unction,
   Also with it a heavenly function,
For after death reviv'd again to lyfe,
This all in all, both husband, child, and wife.

Whilst all is earth conception it is termed,
   And putrefaction tyme of lying in ;
Perfect conjunction (by artes-men is affirm'd)
   The woman's childing where doth all ioy begin :
   Who knows not this his witts are very thin ;
When she is strong and shineth fair and bright
She's tearmed the wife most beautifull to sight.

Loe ; thus you see that you are not beguil'd !
   For, if you mark it, I have proved by reason
How both is one the mother and the child,
   Conception, breeding, childing every season ;
   I have declared to you without all treason,
Or any false ambiguous word at all,
And hewn you worke, then find it true you shall.

This is that Mercury essentiall truly,
   Which is the principall of the Stone materiall,
And not those crude amalgames begun newly—
   These are but Mercuries superficiall ;
   This is that menstrue of perfect tincturial ;
This is most truly that one thing
Out of the which all profitt must springe.

*Edward Kelly :*

If this content you not, abide displeas'd for me,
  For I have done.  If reason takes no place,
What can be said, but that there doubts will
    be,
    Do what one can, where folly wins the race ;
    Let it suffice this is the perfect base,
Which is the Stone that must dissolved be :
How that is done I will declare to thee.

This is the Stone that Ripley bidds you take
  (For untill thus it be it is no stone) :
Be ruled by me, my councell not forsake,
    And he commands, let crudities alone,
    If thou have grace to keep thee free from
      moan.
Then stick to this, let phansey not o'resway thee,
Let reason rule, for phansey will betray thee.

Take thou this Stone, this wife, this child, this
    all,
    Which will be gummous, crumbling, silken,
      soft ;
Upon a glasse or porphire beat it small,
    And, as you grinde, with Mercury feed it oft,
    But not so much that Mercury swim aloft,
But equal parts, nipt up their seed to save ;
Then each in other are buried within their grave.

When thus and there you have it, as is said,
    Worke in all points as Nature wrought at first,
For blacknes had thow needest not be afraid,
    It wil be white, then thou art past the worst,
    Except thou breake thy glass and be accurst ;

But if through blacknes thou to whitenes march,
Then it will be both white and soft as starch.

This very place is cal'd by many names—
  As imbibition, feeding, sublimation,
Clyming high mountaines, also children's games,
  And rightly it is termed exaltation,
  When all is nothing else but circulation
Of the foure elements, whatsoere fooles clatter,
Which is done by heate upon forme and matter.

Earth is the lowest element of all,
  Which black is exalted into water;
Then no more earth but water we it call,
  Although it seeme a black earthy matter,
  And in black dust all about will scatter;
Yet when soe high as to water it hath clym'd
Then it is truly said to be sublym'd.

When this black masse again is become white,
  Both in and out, like snow, and shining faire,
Then this child, this wife, this heaven so bright,
  This water earth sublimed into aire,
  When there it is, it further will prepare
It selfe into the element of fire;
Then give God thankes for granting thy desire.

This black, this white, doe we call seperation,
  Which is not manuall but elementall;
It is no crude mercuriall sublimation,
  But Nature's true worke consubstantiall;
  The white is called conjunction naturall,
Secret and perfect conjunction, not grosse,
Which bringeth profit, all other losse.

When thrice yee have turned this wheele about,
  Feeding and working it as I have said,
Then will it flow like wax without doubt,
  Giving a tincture that will not vade,
  Abiding all tryalls that can be made ;
If wisely project you can and keepe free,
Both profitt and creditt to you it wil be.

Your medicine fixed and perfectly flowing,
  White you must thinke will whitenes increase,
So red begets red, as seede in the sowing
  Begetteth his like, or as kind doth in beasse,
  And fire must be the true maker of peace,
For white or red ferment your medicine aug-
    menteth,
And perfectly tinckteth and soone it relenteth.

That is to say, your medicine ended,
  If white, melt downe silver and thereon
    project it :
If red, melt downe sol, for so it is intended,
  Like unto like, in no wise reject it,
  And out of the purest looke you elect it :
Medicine one part upon ferment ten—
That one on one thousand of Jupiter then.

Your Jupiter standing red hot on the fyre,
  So soon as your medicine upon him is cast,
Presently standeth so hard as a wyre,
  For then he is fixed and melteth by blast,
  And of all your working this is the last ;
Then let it by test or strong water be tryde,
The best gold and silver no better shall bide.

Mercury crude in a crucible heated
Presently hardeneth like silver anealed,
And in the high throwne of Luna is seated.
Silver or gold as medicine hath sealed,
And thus our greate secret I have reveled,
Which divers have seene, and myself have
    wrought
And dearly I prize it, yet give it for nought.

FINIS.— E.K.

---

## SIR ED. KELLEY CONCERNING THE PHILOSOPHER'S STONE.

*Written to his especiall good freind, G. S. Gent.*

---

The heavenly cope hath in him nature's fower—
Two hidden, but the rest to sight appeare :
Wherein the spermes of all the bodies lower
Most secrett are, yett spring forth once a yeare ;
    And as the earth with water, authors are,
    So of his parte is drines end of care.

No flood soe great as that which floweth still,
Nothing more fixt than earth digested thrise,
No winde so fresh as when it serveth will,
No profitt more, then keepe in, and be wise ;
    No better happ, then drie up aire to dust,
    For then thou maist leave of, and sleepe thy
        lust.

Yett will I warne thee, least thou chaunce to
    faile,
Sublyme thine earth with stinkeing water erst ;
Then in a place where Phœbus onely tayle
Is seene att midday, see thou mingle best ;
    For nothing shineth that doth want his light,
    Nor doubleth beames unless it first be bright.

Lett no man lead unless he know the way
That wise men teach, or Adrop leadeth in,
Whereof the first is large and easiest pray,
The other hard and meane but to begin ;
    For surely these and no one more is found
    Wherein Appollo will his harp-strings sound.

Example learne of God that plaste the skyes,
Reflecting virtues from and t'every poynt,
In which the mover wherein all things lyes
Doth hold the vertues all in every joynt,
    And therefore essence fift may well be said,
    Conteining all and yett himselfe a maid

Remember also how the Gods began,
And by discent who was to each the syre ;
Then learne their lives and kingdomes if you
    can,
Their manners eke, with all their whole attire,
    Which if thou do, and know to what effect,
    The learned Sopheis will thee not reject.

If this my doctrine bend not with thy brayne,
Then say I nothing though I said too much ;
Of truth 'tis good will moved me, not gaine,

To write these lynes, yett write I not to such
  As catch at crabs when better fruits appear,
  And what to chuse at fittest time of yeare.

Thou maist (my friend) say, what is this for
    lore ?
I answer such as auncient physicke taught,
And though thou read a thousand bookes before,
Yet in respect of this they teach thee naught :
  Thou mayst likewise be blind and call me
    foole,
  Yet shall these rules for ever praise their
    schoole.

———————

To these very curious specimens of metrical Alchemy it will perhaps be of interest to add one of the shorter tracts which have been attributed to Saint Dunstan. The selection of the following experiments has been governed only by considerations of brevity.

———————

## SAINT DUNSTAN OF THE STONE OF THE PHILOSOPHERS.

———

### I.

Take of the best red transparent ore of gold as much as you can have, and drive its spirit from it through a retort : this is the Azoth and the Acetum of the Philosophers, from its proper minera, which openeth radically Sol that is prepared.

## II.

Take the minera of Venus or Saturn, and drive their spirits in a retort ; each of these dissolveth gold radically, after its purification.

## III.

Take pulverised ore of Saturn, or vulgar Saturn calcined ; extract its salt with Acetum or its antinæ (? *anima*) ; purify it in the best manner, that it may be transparent as crystal, and sweet as honey, and be fluid in heat like wax, and brittle when cold. This is the tree which is cut off, of unwholesome fruits, on which must be inoculated the twigs of Sol.

## IV.

Take of that earth which lieth waste in the field, found everywhere in moorish grounds, into which the astrals ejaculate their operations, being adorned with all manner of colours, appearing like a rainbow ; extract from it its purest and subtilest. This is the universal menstruum for all ; and is all in all.

## V.

Take of the ore of Sol and Mercury a like quantity ; grind each very well ; pour on it the spirit of Mercury, that it stand over three fingers deep. Dissolve and digest it in a gentle warmth.

## VI.

Take of the best vitriol, or of the vitriol of Venus ; drive their spirits in a retort, white and red. With this red spirit, being rectified and sweetened, you may ferment and imbibe the subtle gold calx, and with the white spirit you may dissolve it after it hath been purified.

## VII.

Take quick Mercury ; purify and dissolve it so long in alcolisated spirit of wine, till its impurity be separated from it, and become into its extreme, transparent, easy, fluid essence, like unto the white gluten of the eagle, and capable to receive the blood of the Red Lion.

## VIII.

Extract the salt of the crude and white calcined tartar ; purify and clarify it often, till it be as bright as the tear of the eye, and can be brought no higher ; therewith you may sharpen its own spirit of wine, which dissolveth Sol and Lune.

## IX.

Take of the rank poisonous matter or stone, called kerg swaden, exuviæ, or husk of the metals ; drive its spirit very circumspectly ; receive it so that it may turn unto water ; it reduceth all metals to a potableness.

## X.

Take of the air or heavenly dew, being well purified, ten parts, and of subtle gold calx one part ; set it in digestion, dissolve, and coagulate it.

## XI.

Take the urine of a wholesome man, that drank merely wine ; make of it, according to art, the salt of microcosm ; purify it very well, which doth so much acuate the spirit of wine that it dissolveth Sol in a moment.

## XII.

Take of the best ore of gold ; pulverise it very well ; seal it with Hermes his seal ; set it so long into the vaporous fire till you see it spring up into a white and red rose.

## XIII.

This last experiment he calleth the Light. Take, in the name of the Lord, of Hungarish gold, which hath been cast thrice through antimony and hath been laminated most thinly, as much of it as you will, and make with quick Mercury an amalgam ; then calcine it most subtily, with flowers of sulphur and spirit of wine burnt, so often till there remaineth a subtle gold calx of a purple colour. Take one part of it, and two parts of the above mentioned red matter ; grind it very well together for an hour on a warmed marble ; then cement and calcine well by degrees for three hours in a circle fire. This work must be iterated three times ; then pour on it of the best rectified spirit, that it stand over it three fingers deep ;

set it in a gentle and warm digestion, for six days to be extracted; then the spirit of wine will be tinged as deep as blood; cant off that tincture, and pour on another as long as it will tinge it; put all these tinged spirits of wine into a vial so that the fourth part only be filled, and seal it hermetically; set it on the vaporous fire of the first degree; let it be of that heat as hot as the sun shineth in July; let it stand thus for forty days—then you shall obtain your wish.

The author recommendeth this last experiment very highly, affirming upon his experimental practice that this Aurum Potabile is the highest medicine next unto the universal, and, being taken in appropriated vehicles, cureth all diseases without causing any pains at all.

*Item.*—With this Aurum Potabile is Antimony prepared, so that it purgeth only downward, and carrieth forth all ill humours without molestation, and is called the purging gold.

It is prepared also by the aid of antimony into a diaphoretic gold, to expell by sweating all malignant humours; and Mercurius Vitæ is made also with this Potable Gold (if it be kept in a long digestion); their dose is according to the quality of the person.

## III.

### The Rosicrucians and Doctor Dee.

It is evident from the first section of this notice that Doctor Dee has been popularly regarded as an alchemist with about as much reason as he has also been regarded as a magician. No doubt he knew something of chemistry before he was acquainted with Kelly, and we have seen that he conducted a phenomenal series of experiments in artificial lucidity through the mediation of his celebrated crystal; but he was not an alchemist on the one hand, nor a necromancer and a dealer with devils on the other. He was actually a learned mathematical philosopher, who was to some extent absorbed by the physics and metaphysics of the Hermetic tradition. In particular, he wrote nothing on Alchemy, and it is necessary to accentuate this point, because a hypothesis has been recently put forward which it will not be unreasonable to dispose of in this place. It has been advanced that Doctor Dee was in reality the founder and head of the mysterious Rosicrucian Fraternity, which publicly manifested its existence some twenty years after the death of Edward Kelly, but claimed to have been previously incorporated. Could the philosopher of Mortlake establish his claim to this distinction, it is reasonably clear that his companion must divide with him the honours of having originated one of the most curious historical mysteries. Now, it is well known that, setting aside the imaginative persons who persuade themselves that the Rosicrucians, like the Masonic Brotherhood, can be traced to the period of the Flood, and have disseminated the wild and unaccountable through all ages and in all countries— setting these aside, it is tolerably well known that investigators of the Rosicrucian mystery have cast about them on all sides for some one on whom they could father it. Few mystics of the period have consequently escaped their suspicion. Till recently Dr. Dee—

whether from unsavoury associations, or because he was a little too early— has enjoyed complete immunity ; his turn, however, has arrived, and for a moment it certainly seemed that he was the responsible party. Among the un- published writings of Doctor Dee, some of his biographers have included a manuscript which is preserved in the library of the British Museum, and is devoted to the elucidation of certain Rosicrucian arcana. It has been in- cluded on the faith of the manuscript, which claims to be his composition, but the biographers knew nothing of the Rosicrucian problem, and it passed with- out examination or challenge. Now-a- days, however, people are sufficiently instructed to be aware that if this manuscript must really be ascribed to the author of *Monas Hieroglyphica*, then the Rosicrucians were distinctly in evidence years before the issue of their manifestoes, and they have not unnatu- rally concluded that it is to Dee, as the first exponent of their doctrines, recourse must be had as a likely founder of the Fraternity, and this, in fact, is the latest hypothesis by which it is sought to account for them. The manuscript consists of 501 folios, beautifully written, and illustrated with a few alchemical symbols, Hermetic seals, etc. The slightest examination would shew that it is, at least, not an autograph, for the floriated title contains in a scroll the date March 12th, 1713.* Still it might not incredibly be regarded as a transcript of an original that has been lost; and the criticism which alone could break down this assumption and make evident the imposition which has been practised, would involve a more than common acquaintance with Rosicrucian and alchemical literature. The work is divided into three parts, of which the first is alchemical and medical. It describes the Rosicrucians as without

---

* There is no separate title page. On the right hand of the upper margin is the motto, *Qui vult secreta scire, debet secreta secrete custodire*, and on the left, " The First Sheet of Doctor Dee," which heading continues throughout the first part, a new pagination beginning with the second division.

doubt the wisest of "nations," and affirms that their contemplative order has " presented to the world angels, spirits, planets, and mettals, with the times in astronomy and geomancy to prepare and unite them telesmatically." It quotes Sendivogius and Ripley, Sir Christopher Heydon, etc. On page 201 there is a "Process upon the Philosophical work of Vitriol," with the following marginal note:—"This process Doctor Dee had from Doctor R. set down in a letter, Oct. 19, 1605." There is nothing in the text to indicate that it is communicated matter. It is written, like the rest of the work, mainly in the first person, but lapsing into plurals and imperatives. The references ascribing the entire treatise to Doctor Dee are wholly marginal until folio 352 (b), where the following occurs :— " To conclude these secrets, I shall here insert Doctor John Frederick Helvetius' Letter to Doctor Dee. How in lesse than a quarter of an hour by ye smallest proportion of the Philosopher's Stone, a

great piece of common lead was totally
transmuted into the purest transplen-
dent gold. By Elias Artista." But the
Elias Artista in question was the mysterious adept who imparted the powder of
projection to Helvetius.* The second
part of the manuscript contains an
alphabetical explanation of certain words
hard to be understood, which occur in
the writings of Doctor Dee. The third
part contains a methodical apology for
the Rosicrucian doctrines, and an explanation of the principles which guided
the Fraternity. It may be readily admitted that the manuscript as a whole
is calculated to deceive anyone but a
well-equipped specialist; it is, in fact, a
very curious forgery, rendered the more
difficult to account for by its want of
assignable motive. A critical examination of the first part shews it to be
little else but an adaptation of John

---

* See "John Frederick Helvetius' Golden Calf," trans-
lated in "The Hermetic Museum," Vol. II., p. 271, etc.
This historical transmutation took place at the end of 1666,
more than half a century after the death of Doctor Dee.

Heydon's "Elharvareuna, or Rosicrucian Medicines of Metals," which consists of a dialogue supposed to take
place between Eugenius Philalethes (*i.e.,*
Thomas Vaughan) and Eugenius Theo-
didactus (*i.e.,* Heydon himself). It was
first printed in 1665. The second part
is not definitely traceable to any published work, but there are a variety of
alchemical lexicons, of which it is probably an abridgment ; it is, in any case,
quite certain that the words which it
undertakes to explain are not found in
the extant writings of Doctor Dee. The
third part of the manuscript is an
adapted translation of Michael Maier's
*Themis Aurea,* which appeared in 1618.

Outside the now exploded claim of
this extraordinary imposture, there is
no reason for connecting the philosopher
of Mortlake either remotely or approxi-
mately with the Rosicrucians. At the
same time, it is reasonably within the
limits of this biographical notice to
shortly test the evidence which offers in
the question, because if Dee could be

proved a Rosicrucian, it is fairly certain that Kelly, his inseparable, as well as his inspirer, in Alchemy, must also have been bonded with him in the same brotherhood; and Kelly as a Rosicrucian, connected with the founder of the order, would be undoubtedly of more interest than the "skryer" of Doctor Dee, without prejudice to the philosopher of Mortlake or to the possessor of Saint Dunstan's powder.

ARTHUR EDWARD WAITE.

TO THE MOST POTENT

LORD OF THE HOLY ROMAN EMPIRE,

RUDOLFUS II.,

*King of Hungary and Bohemia, etc.,*
*His Most Gracious Master,*

THIS  BOOK  IS  DEDICATED  BY

EDWARD  KELLY.

# THE STONE

OF THE

# PHILOSOPHERS.

# THE STONE
## OF THE PHILOSOPHERS.

THOUGH I have already twice
suffered chains and imprisonment in Bohemia, an indignity
which has been offered to me in no
other part of the world, yet my mind,
remaining unbound, has all this time
exercised itself in the study of that
philosophy which is despised only by
the wicked and foolish, but is praised
and admired by the wise. Nay, the
saying that none but fools and lawyers
hate and despise Alchemy has passed
into a proverb. Furthermore, as during
the preceding three years I have used
great labour, expense, and care in order
to discover for your Majesty that which
might afford you much profit and
pleasure, so during my imprisonment

—a calamity which has befallen me
through the action of your Majesty—
I am utterly incapable of remaining
idle. Hence I have written a treatise,
by means of which your imperial mind
may be guided into all the truth of the
more ancient philosophy, whence, as
from a lofty eminence, it may contemplate and distinguish the fertile
tracts from the barren and stony
wilderness. But if my teaching dis-
please you, know that you are still
altogether wandering astray from the
true scope and aim of this matter, and
are utterly wasting your money, time,
labour, and hope. A familiar acquaintance with the different branches of
knowledge has taught me this one
thing, that nothing is more ancient,
excellent, or more desirable than truth,
and whoever neglects it must pass his
whole life in the shade. Nevertheless,
it always was, and always will be, the
way of mankind to release Barabbas
and to crucify Christ. This I have—
for my good, no doubt—experienced in

my own case. I venture to hope, however, that my life and character will so become known to posterity that I may be counted among those who have suffered much for the sake of truth. The full certainty of the present treatise time is powerless to abrogate. If your Majesty will deign to peruse it at your leisure, you will easily perceive that my mind is profoundly versed in this study.

(1) All genuine and judicious philosophers have traced back things to their first principles, that is to say, those comprehended in the threefold division of Nature. The generation of animals they have attributed to a mingling of the male and female in sexual union; that of vegetables to their own proper seed; while as the principle of minerals they have assigned earth and viscous water.

(2) All specific and individual things which fall under a certain class, obey the general laws and are referable to the first principles of the class to which they belong.

(3) Thus, every animal is the product of sexual union ; every plant, of its proper seed ; every mineral, of the mixture of its generic earth and water.

(4) Hence, an unchangeable law of Nature regulates the generation of everything within the limits of its own particular genus.

(5) It follows that, with reference to their origin, animals are generically distinct from vegetables and minerals ; the same difference exists respectively between vegetables and minerals and the two other natural kingdoms.

(6) The common and universal matter of these three principles is called Chaos.

(7) Chaos contains within itself the four elements of all that is, viz., fire, air, water, and earth, by the mixture and motion of which the forms of all earthly things are impressed upon their subjects.

(8) These elements have four qualities : heat, coldness, humidity, dryness. The first inheres in fire, the second in

water, the third in air, the fourth in earth.

(9) By means of these qualities, the elements act upon each other, and motion takes place.

(10) Elements either act upon each other, or are acted on, and are called either active or passive.

(11) Active elements are those which, in a compound, impress upon the passive a certain specific character, according to the strength and extent of their motion. These are water and fire.

(12) The passive elements—earth and air — are those which by their inactive qualities readily receive the impressions ˉof the aforesaid active elements.

(13) The four elements are distinguished, not only by their activity and passivity, but also by the priority and posteriority of their motions.

(14) Priority and posteriority are here predicated either with reference to the position of the whole sphere, or

the importance of the result or aim of the motion.

(15) In space, heavy objects tend downwards, and light objects upwards; those which are neither light nor heavy hold an intermediate position.

(16) In this way, even among the passive elements, earth holds a higher place than air, because it delights more in rest; for the less motion, the more passivity.

(17) The excellence of result has reference to perfection and imperfection, the mature being more perfect than the immature. Now, maturity is altogether due to the heat of fire. Hence fire holds the highest place among active elements.

(18) Among the passive elements, the first place belongs to that which is most passive, *i.e.*, which is most quickly and easily influenced. In a compound, earth is first passively affected, then air.

(19) Similarly, in every compound, the perfecting element acts last; for perfection is a transition from immaturity to maturity.

(20) Maturity being caused by heat, cold is the cause of immaturity.

(21) It is clear, then, that the elements, or remote first principles of animals, vegetables, and minerals, in Chaos, are susceptible of active movements in fire and water, and of passive movements in earth and air. Water acts on earth, and transmutes it into its own nature; fire heats air, and also changes it into its own likeness.

(22) The active elements may be called male, while the passive elements represent the female principle.

(23) Any compound belonging to any of these three kingdoms—animal, vegetable, mineral—is female in so far as it is earth and air, and male in so far as it is fire and water.

(24) Only that which has consistency is sensuously perceptible. Elementary fire and air, being naturally subtle, cannot be seen.

(25) Only two elements, water and earth, are visible, and earth is called the hiding-place of fire, water the abode of air.

(26) In these two elements we have the broad law of limitation which divides the male from the female.

(27) The first matter of vegetables is the water and earth hidden in its seed, there being more water than earth.

(28) The first matter of animals is the mixture of the male and female sperm, which embodies more moisture than dryness.

(29) The first matter of minerals is a kind of viscous water, mingled with pure and impure earth.

(30) Impure earth is combustible sulphur, which hinders all fusion, and superficially matures the water joined to it, as we see in the minor minerals, marcasite, magnesia, antimony, etc.

(31) Pure earth is that which so unites the smallest parts of its aforesaid water that they cannot be separated by the fiercest fire, so that either both remain fixed or are volatilized.

(32) Of this viscous water and fusible earth, or sulphur, is composed

that which is called quicksilver, the first matter of the metals.

(33) Metals are nothing but Mercury digested by different degrees of heat.

(34) Different modifications of heat cause, in the metallic compound, either maturity or immaturity.

(35) The mature is that which has exactly attained all the activities and properties of fire. Such is gold.

(36) The immature is that which is dominated by the element of water, and is never acted on by fire. Such are lead, tin, copper, iron, and silver.

(37) Only one metal, viz., gold, is absolutely perfect and mature. Hence it is called the perfect male body.

(38) The rest are immature and, therefore, imperfect.

(39) The limit of immaturity is the beginning of maturity; for the end of the first is the beginning of the last.

(40) Silver is less bounded by aqueous immaturity than the rest of the metals, though it may indeed be

regarded as to a certain extent impure, still its water is already covered with the congealing vesture of its earth, and it thus tends to perfection.

(41) This condition is the reason why silver is everywhere called by the Sages the perfect female body.

(42) All other metals differ only in the degree of their imperfection, according as they are more or less bounded by the said immaturity; nevertheless, all have a certain tendency towards perfection, though they lack the aforesaid · congealing vesture of their earth.

(43) This congealing force is the effect of earthy coldness, balancing its own proper humidity, and causing fixation in the fluid matter.

(44) The lesser metals are fusible in a fierce fire, and therefore lack this perfect congealing force. If they become solid when they cool, this is due to the arrangement of their aforesaid earthy particles.

(45) According to the different ways in which this viscous water and

pure earth are joined together, so as to produce quicksilver by coagulation, with the mediation of natural heat, we have different metals, some of which are called perfect, like gold and silver, while the rest are regarded as imperfect.

(46) Whoever would imitate Nature in any particular operation must first be sure that he has the same matter, and, secondly, that this substance is acted on in a way similar to that of Nature. For Nature rejoices in natural method, and like purifies like.

(47) Hence they are mistaken who strive to elicit the medicine for the tinging of metals from animals or vegetables. The tincture and the metal tinged must belong to the same root or genus; and as it is the imperfect metals upon which the Philosopher's Stone is to be projected, it follows that the powder of the Stone must be essentially Mercury. The Stone is the metallic matter which changes the forms of imperfect metals into gold, as we may learn from the first chapter of " The

Code of Truth " : " The Philosophical Stone is the metallic matter converting the substances and forms of imperfect metals " ; and all Sages agree that it can have this effect only by being like them.

(48) That Mercury is the first matter of metals, I will attempt to prove by the sayings of some Sages.

In the *Turba Philosophorum*, chapter i., we find the following words : " In the estimation of all Sages, Mercury is the first principle of all metals."

And a little further on : " As flesh is generated from coagulated blood, so gold is generated out of coagulated Mercury."

Again, towards the end of the chapter : "All pure and impure metallic bodies are Mercury, because they are generated from the same."

Arnold writes thus to the King of Aragon : " Know that the matter and sperm of all metals are Mercury, digested and thickened in the womb of the earth ; they are digested by sulphureous heat, and according to the quality and quantity of the sulphur different metals are generated. Their matter is essentially the same, though there may be some accidental differences, such as a greater or less degree of digestion, etc. All things are made of that into which they may be resolved, *e.g.*, ice or snow, which may be resolved into water; and so all metals may be resolved into quicksilver; hence they are made out of quicksilver."

The same view is set forth by Bernard of Trevisa, in his book on the "Transmutation of Metals": "Similarly, quicksilver is the substance of all metals; it is as a water by reason of the homogeneity which it possesses with vegetables and animals, and it receives the virtues of those things which adhere to it in decoction." A little further on the same Trevisan affirms that "Gold is nothing but quicksilver congealed by its sulphur."

And, in another place, he writes as follows: "The solvent differs from the soluble only in proportion and degree of digestion, but not in matter, since Nature has formed the one out of the other without any addition, even as by a process equally simple and wonderful she evolves gold out of quicksilver."

Again: "The Sages have it that gold is nothing but quicksilver perfectly digested in the bowels of the earth, and they have signified that this is brought about by sulphur, which coagulates the Mercury, and digests it by its own heat. Hence the Sages have said that gold is nothing but mature quicksilver."

Such also is the concensus of other authorities. "The Sounding of the Trumpet" gives forth no uncertain note: "Extract quicksilver from the bodies, and you have above the ground quicksilver and sulphur of the same substance of which gold and silver are made in the earth."

The "Way of Ways" leads to the same conclusion: "Reverend Father, incline thy venerable ears, and understand that quicksilver is the sperm of all metals, perfect and imperfect, digested in the bowels of the earth by the heat of sulphur, the variety of metals being due to the diversity of their sulphur."

We find in the same tract a similar canon: "All metals in the earth are generated in Mercury, and thus Mercury is the first matter of metals."

To these words Avicenna signifies his assent in chapter iii.: "As ice, which by heat is dissolved into water, is clearly generated out of water, so all metals may be resolved into Mercury, whence it is clear that they are generated out of it."

This reasoning is confirmed by "The Sounding of the Trumpet":— "Every passive body is reduced to its first matter by operations contrary to its nature; the first matter is quicksilver, being itself the oil of all liquid and ductile things."

So also the third chapter of the "Correction of Fools": "The nature of all fusible things is that of Mercury coagulated out of a vapour, or the heat of red or white incombustible sulphur."

In chapter i. of the " Art of
Alchemy" we read: " All Sages agree
that the metals are generated from the
vapour of sulphur and quicksilver."

Again, a passage in the *Turba
Philosophorum* runs thus: " It is certain
that every subject derives from that into
which it can be resolved. All metals
may be resolved into quicksilver, hence
they were once quicksilver."

If it were worth while, I might
adduce hundreds of other passages from
the writings of the Sages, but as they
would serve no good purpose, I will let
these suffice.

Those persons make a great
mistake who suppose that the thick
water of Antimony, or that viscous substance which is extracted from sublimed
Mercury, or from Mercury and Jupiter
dissolved together in a damp spot, can
in any case be the first substance of
metals.

Antimony can never assume
metallic qualities, because its water
and moisture are not tempered with

dry, subtle, earth, and want, moreover, that unctuosity which is characteristic of malleable metals. But, as Chambar well says in the "Code of Truth": "It is only through jealousy that Sages have called the Stone Antimony."

In the same way, those who destroy the natural composition of Mercury, in order to resolve it into a thick or limpid water, which they call the first matter of metals, fight against Nature in the dark, like blinded gladiators.

As soon as Mercury loses its specific form, it becomes something else, which cannot thenceforth mingle with metals in their smallest parts, and is made void for the work of the Philosophers. Whoever is taken up with such childish experiments, should listen to the Sage of Trevisa in his "Transmutation of Metals":

"Who can find truth that destroys the humid nature of Mercury? Some foolish persons change its specific metallic arrangement, corrupt its natural humidity by dissolution, and dispropor

tionate quicksilver from its original
mineral quality, which wanted nothing
but purification and simple digestion.
By means of salts, vitriol, and alum, they
destroy the seed which Nature has been
at pains to develop.  For seed in human
and sensitive things is formed by Nature
and not by art, but by art it is united
and mixed.  Seed needs no addition,
and brooks no diminution.  If it is to
produce a new thing of the same genus,
it must remain the very same thing that
was formed by Nature.  All teaching
that changes Mercury is false and vain,
for this is the original sperm of metals,
and its moisture must not be dried up,
for otherwise it will not dissolve.  Too
much fire will cause a morbid heat, like
that of a fever, and change the passive
into active elements, thus the balance of
forces is destroyed, and the whole work
marred.  Yet these fools extract from
the lesser minerals corrosive waters,
into which they project the different
species of metals, and thus corrode
them.

"The only natural solution is that by which out of the solvent and the soluble, or male and female, there results a new species. No water can naturally dissolve metals except that which abides with them in substance and form, which also the dissolved metals can again congeal; this is not the case with *aqua fortis*, seeing that it only destroys the specific arrangement. Only that water can rightly dissolve metals which is inseparable from them in fixation, and such a water is Mercury, but not *aqua fortis*, or any thing else which those fools are pleased to call Mercurial Water." Thus far Trevisan.

Persons who have fallen into this fatal error may also derive benefit from the teaching of Avicenna on this point: "Quicksilver is cold and humid, and of it, or with it, God has created all metals. It is aërial, and becomes volatile by the action of fire, but when it has withstood the fire a little time, it accomplishes great marvels, and is itself only a living spirit of unexampled potency. It enters and penetrates all bodies, passes through them, and is their ferment. It is then the White and the Red Elixir and is an everlasting water, the water of life, the Virgin's milk, the spring, and that Alum of which whosoever drinks cannot die, etc. It is the wanton serpent that conceives of its own seed, and brings forth on the same day. With its poison it destroys all things. It is volatile, but the wise make it to abide the fire, and then it transmutes as it has been transmuted, and tinges as it has been tinged, and coagulates as it has been coagulated. Therefore is the generation of quicksilver to be preferred before all minerals; it is found in all ores, and has its sign with all. Quicksilver is that which saves metals from combustion, and renders them fusible. It is the Red Tincture which enters into the most intimate union with metals, because it is of their own nature, mingles with them indissolubly in all their smallest parts, and, being homogeneous, naturally adheres to them. Mercury receives all homogeneous substances, but rejects all that is heterogeneous, because it delights in its own nature, but recoils from whatsoever is strange. How foolish, then, to spoil and destroy that which Nature made the seed of all metallic virtue by elaborate chemical operations!"

The "Rosary" bids us be particularly careful, lest in purifying the quicksilver we dissipate its virtue, and impair its active force. A grain of wheat, or any other seed, will not grow if its generative virtue be destroyed by excessive external heat. Therefore, purify your quicksilver by distillation over a gentle fire.

Says the Sage of Trevisa: "If the quicksilver be robbed of its due metallic proportion, how can other substances of the same metallic genus be generated from it? It is a mistake to suppose that you can work miracles with a clear limpid water extracted from quicksilver. Even if we could get such a water, it would not be of use, either as to form or proportion, nor could it restore or build up a perfect metallic species. For as soon as the quicksilver is changed from its first nature, it is rendered unfit for our operation, since it loses its spermatic and metallic quality. I do, indeed, approve of impure and gross Mercury being sublimed and purified once or twice with simple salt, according to the proper method of the Sages, so long as the fluxibility or radical humour of such Mercury remains unimpaired, that is to say, so long as its specific mercurial nature is not destroyed, and so long as its outward appearance does not become that of a dry powder."

In the " Ladder of the Sages " we are told to beware of vitrification in the solution of bodies, with the odour and taste of imperfect substances, and also of the generative virtue of their form being in any way scorched and destroyed by corrosive waters.

If you have been trying to do any of these things, you may see how grievous your mistake has been. For the water of the Sages adheres to nothing except homogeneous substances. It does not wet your hands if you touch it, but scorches your skin, and frets and corrodes every substance with which it comes in contact, except gold and silver (it would not affect these until they have been dissipated and dissolved by spirits and strong waters), and with these it combines most intimately. But the other mixture is most childish, it is condemned by the concert of the Sages, and by my own experience.

I now propose to shew that quicksilver is the water with which, and in which, the solution of the Sages takes place, by putting before the reader the opinions of many Philosophers living in different countries and ages.

Says Menalates in the *Turba*: " Whoever joins quicksilver to the body of magnesia, and the woman to the man, extracts the hidden nature by which bodies are coloured. Know that

quicksilver is a consuming fire which
mortifies bodies by its contact."

Another Sage, in the *Turba*,
says : " Divide the elements by fire,
unite them through the mediation of
Mercury, which is the greatest arcanum, and so the magistery is complete, the whole difficulty consisting in
the solution and conjunction. The
solution, or separation, takes place
through the mediation of Mercury,
which first dissolves the bodies, and
these are again united by ferment and
Mercury."

Rosinus makes Gold address Mercury as follows : " Dost thou dispute
with me, Mercury ? I am the Lord,
the Stone which abides the fire." Says
Mercury : " Thou sayest true ; but I
have begotten thee, and one part of me
quickens many of thee, since thou art
grudging in comparison with me. Whoever will join me to my brother or sister
shall live and rejoice, and make me
sufficient for thee."

In the 5th chapter of the " Book of

Three Words," we read: " I tell thee
that in Mercury are the works of the
planets, and all their imaginations in its
pages."

Aristotle says that the first mode
of preparation is that the Stone shall
become Mercury ; he calls Mercury the
first body, which acts on gross substances and changes them into its own
likeness. " If Mercury did nothing else
than render bodies subtle and like itself,
it would suffice us."

Senior: " Our Stone, then, is congealed water, that is to say, Mercury
congealed in gold and silver, and, when
fixed, resistent to the fire."

" The Sounding of the Trumpet " :
" Mercury contains all that the Sages
seek, and destroys all flaky gold. It
dissolves, softens, and extracts the soul
from the body."

" The Book on the Art of Alchemy " : " The Sages were first put
upon attempting to clothe inferior bodies
in the glory and splendour of the perfect
body when they discovered that metals

differ only according to the greater or smaller degree of their digestion, and are all generated from Mercury, with which they extracted gold and reduced it to its first nature."

The " Correction of Fools " : " Observe that crude Mercury dissolves bodies and reduces them to their first matter or nature. Being made of clear water, it always strives to corrode the crude, and especially that which is nearest to its own nature, viz., gold and silver." The same book observes : " You can make use of crude Mercury as follows—to seal up and open natures, since similar things are helpful one to another." Once more : " Quicksilver is the root in the Art of Alchemy, for the Sages say that all metals are of it, and through it, and in it—it follows that the metals must first be reduced to Mercury, the matter and sperm of all metals."

Again : " The reason why all metals must be reduced to the nature of vapour is because we see that all are generated of quicksilver, through the mediation of which they came into being."

Gratianus : " Purify Laton, *i.e.*, copper (ore), with Mercury, for Laton is of gold and silver, a compound, yellow, imperfect body."

" The Sounding of the Trumpet ": " Common Mercury is called a spirit. If you do not resolve the body into Mercury, with Mercury, you cannot obtain its hidden virtue."

" Art of Alchemy," chapter vi. : " The second part of the Stone we call living Mercury, which, being living and crude, is said to dissolve bodies, because it adheres to them in their innermost being. This is the Stone without which Nature does nothing."

" Rosary ": " Mercury never dies, except with its brother and sister. When Mercury mortifies the matter of the Sun and Moon, there remains a matter like ashes."

The Sage of Trevisa : " Add nothing above ground for digesting and thickening Mercury into the nature of gold or of metals." Again : "This solution is possible and natural, that is to say, by Art as handmaid to Nature, and is unique and necessary in the work ; but it is brought about only by quicksilver, in such proportions as commend themselves to a good workman who knows the inmost properties of Nature."

"Art of Alchemy" : "Who can sufficiently extol Mercury, for Mercury alone has power to reduce gold to its first nature ? "

From these quotations it is clear what the Sages meant by their water, and what they thought of this wonderful liquid, viz., Mercury, to which they ascribed all power in the Magistery, for nothing can be perfected outside its own genus. Men digest vegetables, not in the blood of animals, but in water which is their first principle, nor are minerals affected by the vegetable liquid. In the words of the "Sounding of the Trumpet" : "The whole Magistery consists in dividing the elements from the metals, and purifying them, and in separating the sulphur of Nature from the metals."

Furthermore, as Hermes says, only homogeneous substances cohere, and only they can produce offspring after their own kind, *i.e.*, if you want a medicine which is to generate metals, its origin must be metallic, since " species are tinged by their genus," as the philosopher testifies.

In short, our whole Magistery consists in the union of the male and female, or active and passive, elements through the mediation of our metallic water and a proper degree of heat. Now, the male and female are two metallic bodies, and this I will again prove by irrefragable quotations from the Sages :

Dantius bids us prepare the bodies and dissolve them.

Rhasis : " Change the bodies into water, and the water into earth : then all is done."

Galienus : " Prepare the bodies, and purify them of the blackness in which is corruption, till the white becomes white and red, then dissolve both, etc."

Calid (chapter i.) : " If you do not make the bodies subtle, so that they may be impalpable to touch, you will not gain your end. If they have not been ground, repeat your operation, and see that they are ground and subtilized. If you do this, you will be directed to your desired goal."

Aristotle : " Bodies cannot be changed except by reduction into their first matter."

Calid (chapter v.) : " Similarly, the Sages have commanded us to dissolve the bodies so that heat adheres to their inmost parts; then we proceed to coagulation after a second dissolution with a substance which most nearly approaches them."

Menabadus : " Make bodies not bodies, and incorporeal things bodies, for this is the whole process by which the hidden virtue of Nature is extracted."

Ascanius: " The conjunction of the two is like the union of husband and wife, from whose embrace results golden water."

"Anthology of Secrets": " Wed the red man to the white woman, and you have the whole Magistery."

" The Sounding of the Trumpet " : "There is another quicksilver and permanent tincture which is extracted from perfect bodies by dissolution, distillation, sublimation, and subtilization."

Hermes : " Join the male to the female in their own proper humidity, because there is no birth without union of male and female."

Plato : " Nature follows a kindred nature, contains it, and teaches it to resist the fire. Wed the man to the woman, and you have the whole Magistery."

Avicenna : " Purify husband and wife separately, in order that they may unite more intimately; for if you do not purify them, they cannot love each other. By conjunction of the two natures you get a clear and lucid nature, which, when it ascends, becomes bright and serviceable."

"Art of Alchemy": "Two bodies provide us with everything in our water."

Trevisanus: "Only that water which is of the same species, and can be thickened by bodies, can dissolve bodies."

Hermes : "Let the stones of mixture be taken in the beginning of the first work, and let them be equally mixed into earth."

"Mirror": "Our Stone must be extracted from the nature of two bodies, before it can become a perfect Elixir."

Democritus: "You should first dissolve the bodies over white hot ashes, and not grind them except only with water."

"Rosary" of Arnold: "Extract the Medicine from the most homogeneous bodies in Nature."

I have thus proved the number of the bodies from which the Elixir is obtained. I will now shew by quotations what these bodies are.

"Exposition of the Letter of King Alexander": "In this art you must wed the Sun and the Moon."

"The Sounding of the Trumpet": "The Sun only heats the earth and imparts to it his virtue through the mediation of the Moon, which, of all stars, most readily receives his light and heat."

"The Correction of Fools": "Sow gold and silver, and they will yield to your labour a thousandfold, through the mediation of that thing which alone has what you seek. The Tincture of gold and silver exhibits the same metallic proportions as the imperfect metals, because they have a common first matter in Mercury."

Again: "Tinge with gold and silver, because gold gives the golden and silver the silver colour and nature. Reject all things that have not naturally or virtually the power of tinging, as in them is no fruit, but only waste of money and gnashing of teeth."

Senior: " I, the Sun, am hot and dry, and thou, the Moon, art cold and moist; when we are wedded together in a closed chamber, I will gently steal away thy soul."

Rosinus to Saratant: " From the living water we obtain earth, a homogeneous dead body, composed of two natures, that of the Sun and that of the Moon."

Again : " When the Sun, my brother, for the love of me (silver) pours his sperm (*i.e.* his solar fatness) into the chamber (*i.e.,* my Lunar body), namely, when we become one in a strong and complete complexion and union, the child of our wedded love will be born."

Hermes : "Its humidity is of the empire of the Moon, and its fatness of the empire of the Sun, and these two are its coagulum and pure seed."

Astratus says : " Whoever would attain the truth, let him take the humour of the Sun and the Spirit of the Moon."

*Turba Philosophorum:* "Both bodies in their perfection should be taken for the composition of the Elixir, whether orange or white, for neither becomes liquid without the other."

Again, Gold says: " No one kills me but my sister."

Aristotle: " If I did not see gold and silver, I should certainly say that Alchemy was not true."

The Sage : " The foundation of our Art is gold and its shadow."

" Art of Alchemy ": " We have already said that gold and silver must be united."

" Rosary ": " There is an addition of orange colour by which the Medicine is perfected from the substance of fixed sulphur, *i e.*, both medicines are obtained from gold and silver."

The Sage : " Whoever knows how to tinge sulphur and quicksilver has reached the great arcanum. Gold and silver must be in the Tincture, and also the ferment of the spirit."

" Rosary ": " The ferment of the Sun is the sperm of the man, the fer· ment of the Moon, the sperm of the woman. Of both we get a chaste union and a true generation."

"The Sounding of the Trumpet": "You want silver to subtilize your gold, and make it volatile by removing its impurity, since the silver has a greater need of the light of gold. Therefore Hermes, as also Aristotle in his treatise on Plants, says that gold is its father, and silver its mother; nothing else is needed for our Stone. Silver is the field in which the seed of gold is sown." And a little further on: "In my sister, the Moon, grows your wisdom, and not in any other of my servants, saith the Lord Sun. I am like seed sown in good and pure soil, which sprouts and grows and multiplies and yields great gain to the sower. I, the Sun, give to thee, the Moon, my beauty, the light of the Sun, when we are united in our smallest parts." And the Moon says to the Sun: "Thou hast need of me, as the cock has need of the hen, and I need thy operation, who art perfect in morals, the father of lights, a great and mighty lord, hot and dry, and I am the waxing Moon, cold and moist, but I receive thy nature by our union."

Avicenna : " In order to obtain the red and the white Elixir, the two bodies must be united. For though gold is the most fixed and perfect of the metals, yet if it be dissolved into its smallest parts, it becomes spiritual and volatile, like quicksilver, and that because of its heat. This tincture, which is without number, is called the hot male seed. But if silver be dissolved in warm water, it remains fixed as before, and has little or no tincture, yet it readily receives the tincture in a temperament of hot and cold, and is called the cold, dry, female seed. Gold or silver by themselves are not easily fusible, but a mixture of the two melts readily, as is well known to goldsmiths. Hence if our Stone did not contain both gold and silver, it would not be liquid, and would yield no medicine through any magistery, nor tincture, for if it yielded tincture it would still have no tinging power."

And a little further on: "Take heed, then, and operate only on gold, silver, and quicksilver, since all the profit of our Art is derived from these three."

I may add that crude Mercury is the water which the Sages have used for the purpose of solution. I have proved that two bodies must be dissolved, and that they are no other than gold and silver. Now I will describe the conjunction of these two bodies by means of the crude Mercury of the Sages.

"The Light of Lights": "Know that it is gold, silver, and Mercury that whiten and redden within and without. The Dragon does not die, unless he be killed with his brother and sister, and it must be not by one, but by both together."

"The Ladder of the Sages": "Others say that a true body must be added to these two, to strengthen and shorten the operation."

"Treasury of the Sages": "Our

Stone has body, soul, and spirit, the imperfect body is the body, the ferment the soul, and the water the spirit."

"The Way of Ways": "The water is called the spirit, because it gives life to the imperfect and mortified body, and imparts to it a better form; the ferment is the soul, because it gives life to the body, and changes it into its own nature."

Again: "The whole Magistery is accomplished with our water, and of it. For it dissolves the bodies, calcines and reduces them to earth, transforms them into ashes, whitens and purifies them, as Morienus says: "Azoth and fire purify Laton, that is to say, wash it and thoroughly remove its obscurity; Laton is the impure body, Azoth is quicksilver."

"The Sounding of the Trumpet": "As without the ferment there is no perfect tincture, as the Sages say, so without leaven there is no good bread. In our Stone the ferment is like the soul, which gives life to the dead body

through the mediation of the spirit,
or Mercury."

"The Rosary" and Peter of
Zalentum say: "If the ferment, which is
the medium of conjunction, be placed in
the beginning, or in the middle, the
work is more quickly perfected."

"The Sounding of the Trumpet":
"The Elixir of the Sages is composed
of three things, viz., the Lunar, the
Solar, and the Mercurial Stone. In the
Lunar Stone is white sulphur, in the
Solar Stone red sulphur, and the
Mercurial Stone embraces both, which
is the strength of the whole Magis-
tery."

Eximenus : "The water, with its
adjuncts, being placed in the vessel,
preserves them from combustion.
The substances being ground with
water, there follows the ascension of the
Ethelia and the imbibition of water is
sufficient by itself to complete the work."

Plato: "Take fixed bodies, join
them together, wash the body in the
bodily substance, and let it be strength-

ened with the incorporeal body, till you change it into a real body."

Pandulphus : " The fixed water is pure water of life, and no tinging poison is generated without gold and its shadow. Whoever tinges the poison of the Sages with the Sun and its shadow, has attained the highest wisdom."

Again : " Separate the elements with fire, unite them by means of Mercury, and the Magistery is complete."

Exercit, 14 : " The spirit guards the body and preserves it from fire, the clarified body keeps the spirit from evaporating over the fire, the body being fixed and the spirit incombustible. Hence the body cannot be burnt, because the body and spirit are one through the soul. The soul prevents them from being separated by the fire. Hence the three together can defy the fire and anything else in the world."

Rhasis (" Book of Lights ") : " Our Stone is named after the creation of the world, being three and yet one. Nowhere is our Mercury found purer than in gold, silver, and common Mercury."

When bodies and spirits are dissolved, they are resolved into the four elements, which become a firm and fixed substance. But when they are not both dissolved, there is a particular mixture which the fire can still separate.

Rosinus : " In our Magistery are a spirit and bodies, whence it is said: It rejoices being sown in the three associated substances."

Calid : " Prepare the strong bodies with the dissolved humidity, till either shall be reduced to its subtle form. If you do not subtilize and grind the bodies till they become impalpable, you will not find what you seek."

Rosinus: " The Stone consists of body, soul, and spirit, or water, as the Philosophers say, and is digested in one vessel. Our whole Magistery is of, and by, our water, which dissolves the bodies, not into water, but by a true philosophical solution into the water whence metals are extracted, and is calcined and reduced to earth. It makes yellow as wax those bodies into whose nature it is transformed; it substantialises, whitens, and purifies the Laton, according to the word of Morienus."

Aristotle : " Take your beloved son, and wed him to his sister, his white sister, in equal marriage, and give them the cup of love, for it is a food which prompts to union. All pure things must be united to pure things, or they will have sons unlike themselves. Therefore, first of all, even as Avicenna advises, sublime the Mercury, and purify in it impure bodies. Then pound and dissolve. Repeat this operation again and again."

Ascanius : " Stir up war between copper and Mercury till they destroy each other and devour each other. Then the copper coagulates the quicksilver, the quicksilver congeals the copper, and both bodies become a powder by means of diligent imbibition and digestion. Join together the red man and the white woman till they become Ethelia, that is, quicksilver. Whoever changes them into a spirit by means of quicksilver, and then makes them red, can tinge every body."

As to the nature of this copper, Gratianus instructs us in the following words : " Make Laton white, *i.e.*, whiten copper with Mercury, because Laton is an orange imperfect body, composed of gold and silver."

I advise all and sundry to follow my teaching, as to the correctness of which my quotations from the ancients can leave no doubt, which also has received further confirmation from my own experiments. Any deviation from this course leads to deception, except only the work of Saturn, which must be performed by the subtilization of principles. The Sages say that homogeneous things only combine with each other, make each other white and red, and permit of common generation. The important

point is that Mercury should act upon
our earth. This is the union of male
and female, of which the Sages say so
much. After the water, or quicksilver,
has once appeared, it grows and in-
creases, because the earth becomes
white, and this is called the impreg-
nation. Then the ferment is coagulated, *i.e.*, joined to the imperfect prepared body, till they become one in
colour and appearance : this is termed
the birth of our Stone, which the Sages
call the King. Of this substance it is
said in the " Art of Alchemy" that if
any one scorches this flower, and separates the elements, the generative germ
is destroyed.

I conclude with the words of Avicenna: "The true principle of our
work is the dissolution of the Stone,
because solved bodies have assumed
the nature of spirits, *i.e.*, because their
quality is drier. For the solution of
the body is attended with the coagulation of the spirit. Be patient, therefore,
digest, pound, make yellow as wax, and

never be weary of repeating these processes till they are quite perfect. For
things saturated with water are thereby
softened. The more you pound the
substance, the more you soften it, and
subtilize its gross parts, till they are
thoroughly penetrated with the spirit
and thus dissolved. For by pounding,
roasting, and fire, the tough and viscous
parts of bodies are separated."

Finally, I do you to wit, sons of
knowledge, that in the work of the Sages
there are three solutions.

The first is that of the crude body.

The second is that of the earth of
the Sages.

The third is that which takes place
during the augmentation of the substance. If you diligently consider all
that I have said, this Magistery will
become known to you. As for me, how
much I have endured on account of this
Art, history will reveal to future ages.

# SOME FRAGMENTS OF KELLY.

## EXTRACTED FROM HIS LETTERS.

—————

[*From a letter of Edward Kelly, dated
June* 20, 1587.]

AS you are willing to take my advice, I will partially reveal to you the Arcanum, so that the field may not disappoint the hopes of the husbandman. Open your ears. Our gold and silver, Sun and Moon, active and passive principles, are not those which you can hold in your hand, but a certain silver and golden hermaphroditic water; if you extract it from any perfect or imperfect metallic body, you have the Water of Life, the Asafœtida, and Green Lion, in which are all colours, ending in two—white and red. The earth does not so much matter, only let it be fixed, for the Elixir must above all be fixed. If you are in

earnest, all your thoughts must be con-
centrated on the fixed earth and the
indestructible metallic water ; nor need
you seek these in gold or silver, or in
any determinate compound. It is true,
however, that after the separation of
this tincture from the gold, that indes-
.tructible water is fixed in its white
earth ; but it is foolish to do by much
what you can do by little.

[*From a letter dated August* 9, 1587.]

The Sages agree that the Stone is
nothing but animated quicksilver. But
if your quicksilver has no life, it is not
what they mean. Again, if it has the
form of Mercury, before it receives life,
it is unprofitable. For this woman— to
be more frank than discreet—is a
viscous water, extracted from the bowels
of Jupiter, *i.e.,* from white lead ; it is
moist and wets the finger. If a proper
quantity of the body of the Sun is added
to it, it is coagulated and becomes
brilliant,—the Sun is dissolved into
exceedingly limpid mineral water. For

the water dissolves the Sun at the very same moment that itself is congealed, and thus the solution of one is the co-agulation of the other, at the very same instant. This compound is living Mercury, from which alone spring all colours. To regulate the fire is mere child's play. After the conjunction it looks just like common limpid Mercury, and does not moisten the finger but is viscous and living.

[*From a letter dated Nov.* 15, 1589.]

I have given you both luminaries and the best instruction concerning these things, if you can bear it in mind. To sum it all up in a few words : " Mix water with water, digest with a vaporous cloud, and you will not easily make a mistake."

# EDWARD KELLY'S

# HUMID PATH,

OR

## DISCOURSE ON THE

## VEGETABLE MENSTRUUM

## OF SATURN.

[FROM A MANUSCRIPT.]

# THE HUMID PATH.

P LATO has justly defined philosophers as men who contemplate
with wonder the marvellous
works of Nature in all parts of the
created universe ; who study the size,
properties, movements, courses, and
revolutions of the heavens and their
flaming worlds, their rising, setting,
priority, and posteriority of appearance,
rate of progress, irregularities, stop-
pages, velocity, and the seeds and principles, dimensions and tendencies of all
sublunar bodies. By their constant
desire and thirst for knowledge they are
impelled not only intellectually to apprehend the mysteries and great arcana of
Nature, but also to imitate and even to
improve upon them, as may be deduced
with the greatest ease from so many

hieroglyphical writings, magical and
mathematical mysteries, and all the
other marks of the antiquity of philosophy.  Nay, it seems absurd that men
highly distinguished in letters, and after
filling the highest offices in the State,
should retire from public life for the
sake of a childish study, neglect the
splendour of worldly fame, and the hope
of riches,-- a course they would never
have adopted if they had really regarded
this Art as diametrically opposed to the
laws of Nature.  All these men firmly
believed in the possibility of enjoying
for many years a sound mind in a sound
body, and this desirable result they con-
sidered as attainable only by the discovery of the central substance in which
all the forces and virtues of Nature meet,
following the royal road and philosophical method.  They knew, indeed, that
the mind is the most celestial, divine,
pure, subtle, immortal, omniscient part
of man, being receptive of God.  But
they also knew that the body, its dingy
workshop of frail clay, obscures its move-

ments, enfeebles its powers, and prevents it from expanding in a way worthy
of itself. They knew that some means
was needed whereby all superfluity might
be curtailed, all imperfections matured,
all weak things strengthened, all solid
things confirmed, so that the whole structure might rejoice in an assured and
continuous perfection. But in order to
attain this end, they knew that they must
have a minute and detailed acquaintance with the elements of the human
body and of the universe generally.
Before they could discover the cause of
perfection, they must first study the
nature of the elements. The Sages saw
that the instrument toward the attain-
ment of their purpose was a good knowledge of physical arts and sciences.
After having conceived in their minds a
Divine idea of the relations of the whole
universe, they selected from among the
rest a certain substance, from which
they sought to elicit the elements, to
separate and purify them, and then
again put them together in a manner

suggested by a keen and profound
observation of Nature. Thus, they obtained a body freed from all imperfections and impurities, which, being
disclosed by their careful operation and
due regard to times and seasons,
afforded not only health to their physical nature, but the highest delight and
instruction to their minds. These facts
were first brought out by Hermes
Trismegistus in his famous Emerald
Table, and the truth of this assertion is
borne out by the unanimous testimony
of antiquity, and the consensus of the
most illustrious men of all ages. That
the aspiration of our Art is no Utopian
dream, is proved by the innumerable
and stupendous metamorphoses which
Nature daily exhibits on every side.
The Sages have, indeed, purposely con-
cealed their meaning under a veil of
obscure words, but it is sufficiently clear
from their writings that the substance
of which they speak is not of a special,
but a general kind, and is therefore
contained in animals, vegetables, and

minerals. It would, however, be unwise
to take a round-about road where there
is a shorter cut; and they say that
whereas the substance can be found in
the animal and vegetable kingdoms
only with great difficulty, and at the cost
enormous labour, in the bowels of the
earth it lies ready to our hands. It
is the matter which the Sages have
agreed to call Mercury or Quicksilver.
Our quicksilver, indeed, is truly a living
substance, so-called not because it is
extracted from cinnabar, but because it
is derived from the metals themselves.
If common Mercury be freed by fixation
from its crude, volatile, and watery
superfluities, it may, with the aid of our
Art, attain to the purity and virtue of
the substance of which we speak. And
as this Mercury is the metallic basis
and first substance, it may be found in
all metals whatsoever. Other wise,
learned, and sagacious men, who in
perusing the books of the Sages failed
to pay attention to this fact, have
wasted both their time and their labour.

Nothing contributes so much to a ready
apprehension of our secret as a knowledge of our first substance, and after
that of the distinctive species of minera
which is the subject of investigation by
the Philosopher. You should learn that
the earth is the mother of the elements,
and that their arrangements and pro-
portionate mixture are that which constitutes the difference between one
species and another. Of these elements
two, viz., fire and water, are active,
while two, earth and air, are passive.
Fire and water strive to unite themselves to earth, but can do so only
by means of the qualities which they
have in common with it, *i.e.*, in the
case of fire, dryness, and, in the case
of water, coldness. So fire and water
introduce themselves into earth by
means of their dryness and coldness,
and into air by means of their heat
and moisture. Now, according as
earth is more or less dry or cold, its
centre will be occupied either by fire or
water, while the other active element

will be confined to its circumference.
In the former case, the inborn dryness
or heat of the fire being invisible and
intangible, and residing, as it were, at
the heart of the earth, will escape observation, but the humidity of the water,
being more tangible and nearer to the
surface, will be more easily noticed.
The surface of this compound will thus
be watery, cold, and dry; and such is
the substance which is commonly called
quicksilver. But it should be borne in
mind that no account has been taken of
the air that surrounds and, as it were,
adheres to the earth in which fire and
water are striving for the mastery. If
the fire conquers the water, it will ex-
tend its operation to the air with which
it has heat in common, and the exuberant strength of their united heat will
subdue the humidity of the air, and
impress upon it a new form of excessive
dryness. The preponderance of fire
will cause the colour of that element
to tinge the whole substance, and thus
we have that which is commonly called

sulphur. But if in the above case the water (in the earth) subdues the fire, it insinuates itself into the air by means of its humidity, and subdues to itself the heat of the air; now, as it is the property of cold to congeal, and this cold has been increased by that of the earth, there results a substance of icy whiteness which is called salt. These three (Mercury, Sulphur, Salt) are necessarily the first substances of all minerals, and every mineral must be generated from one, or two, or all of them. But minerals do not consist of salt, sulphur, and mercury, as of parts which introduce the form, as some learned men have vainly supposed. For, in that case, such minerals would necessarily receive one or more of those forms in succession before they could be clothed with another. Rather they derive their being from one or more of these principles in different proportions as from their own proper source. For as the numbers 2, 3, and 4, are the foundation (of other numbers), though they them-

selves consist partly of units and partly
of each other, as, for instance, 12 contains within itself 3 times 4, 4 times 3,
6 times 2, and 12 times 1, which are,
nevertheless, all lost in its own proper
name — so Mercury, Sulphur, and Salt,
exist sometimes singly, sometimes in
couples, and sometimes jointly, in
mineral bodies. And as 3, the fourth
part of 12, consists of 3 units, or of 2
and 1 unit, while it is included in 4,
which exceeds it by 1 unit, so some
minerals which derive their motive force
from a simple union of fire, water, and
and earth (which union, as aforesaid,
constitutes Mercury), have no affinity
with Sulphur or Salt, the perfection of
which arises from the addition of air,
the fourth element. Here the question
naturally arises whether Mercury contains Sulphur, and I say that, in the
vulgar sense of that word-—viz., in the
sense of combustible sulphur—it does
not. But how then are we to understand the sayings of the ancient Sages,
according to whom every metal contains

its own sulphur, or naturally fixed
earth, which is the cause of all fixation,
a constituent and fundamental element
of Mercury? Nature has produced
only two visible elements, the one
active, the other passive, earth and
water, in which the others, fire and air,
which are naturally invisible and intangible, have their domicile and abode.
We can know only these outward and
visible elements; the bonds of the other
elements can be loosed, and their
presence ascertained, only by the ingenious contrivances of art. Hence
fire may be contained in a substance,
even if it be not seen—and, to return to
our enquiry, if in quicksilver by itself
there is no combustible sulphur, but
only a certain fixed earth, by which
Mercury receives life, I am quite willing
to call this fixed earth sulphur. For if
all elements have a common substance,
and are only forms, out of which,
through intermixture and mutual action,
other forms may be generated, surely
fire, being superficially bounded by

water (which was stated to be the case
with Mercury), will throw out rays from
the centre, and penetrate the whole
substance with its sulphureous nature.
The animation, or quickening, of Mercury is nothing but a purification of all
parts by fire, the result of which is the
formation of sulphur. The correctness
of this explanation is shewn by intro-
ducing artificial heat into common
Mercury; for then the innate central
fire, being drawn towards the circumference, changes in a few weeks that
mercurial crudity into red sparkling
sulphur. For all elements are the
bases of certain colours, of which blackness and whiteness are associated respectively with earth and water, while
the rest are called intermediate colours.
When earth has in perfection all its
qualities of coldness, dryness, solidity,
ponderosity, firmness, stability, and
obscurity, there results a colour which
is specifically represented by all the
shades between black and tawny.
After earth comes water, like the first,

cold in its nature, but also humid, full
of fluxional lines and figures, and the
nurse of temperament.  The leading
colour of water is whiteness, its species
all the shades between white and grey.
The air is more passive and liable to
the incursions of fire and water; it is
lightened and attenuated, has no proper
colour, but is tinged by the heat rays;
its whiteness is often more intense than
that of water, and in the course of the
day it reflects all the shades between
lilac and a kind of yellow.  Fire, being
hot and dry, pure, simple, subtle, rare,
thin, and bright, represents all ruddy
colours between the limits of yellow
and the deep red of twice digested
blood.  These colours the Sages have
used as a kind of cynosure to steer their
course throughout Nature, and especially in the investigation of the
secret Medicine.  In the preparation of
this arcanum we must study not only
the arrangements of bodies, their proportions, qualities, and motions, but also
their fundamental constituent principles,

as Salt, Sulphur, and Quicksilver, as
also all parts of the ore; nor is it
sufficient to know that Mercury is a
principle which is contained in all
animals, vegetables, and minerals; you
must also know what it is, how com-
pounded, its length, width, and depth,
and what effects it produces when
joined to other bodies. In all these
researches the knowledge of colours is
most important. The Sages never
tire of inculcating the truth that this
quicksilver is found in animals and
vegetables; and it is most unwise to
contradict their assertion. For if animals, vegetables, and minerals contain
within themselves water and earth,
which embrace the other elements, it is
clear that in all things there are the
same principles. Hence, wherever there
are water and earth, every form is
potentially present, and we may look for
Mercury, Sulphur, and Salt. For as the
number one enters into all numbers, so
it is with the constituent principles of
matter; every compound substance, be-

sides its own form, contains within itself
all the conditions and causes of that
form. This principle of mixture is
most highly developed in the case of
minerals, and least in the case of vegetables. Now, animals and vegetables
are higher organisations than minerals,
and contain all that is in minerals.
Hence Salt, Sulphur, and Mercury are
contained in animals, vegetables, and
minerals. In animal ashes, or animal
earth (which is a product of the vegetable world), we find these three principles. For if we pour on them water,
we extract salt; if we dry them, and
subject them to the action of a fierce
fire, there follows a fusion into a glassy
substance, from which the Sages can
extract Mercury; and if in this Mercury
the rays of the central fire are drawn
towards the circumference, it is quickened, and penetrated with the form of
sulphur. Again, let us divide salt by
our art into its parts, water and earth;
and do the same with Sulphur and Mercury. You have nothing but water and

earth ; but water and earth contain air and fire, and so we have the same elements in every case. Salt, Sulphur, and Mercury do indeed differ in outward form according to the different proportions of their mixture, but they consist of the same elements which are the first principles of all creation. This is the universal sperm of Anaxagoras. who said that all things had the same first substance ; it is only through a misunderstanding that Aristotle attacked his system.

Hence we see that the matter of our Stone, Mercury, is a commonly diffused subject, and though it is found with greater ease in some minerals, it may be discovered everywhere. In this sense Morienus, that illustrious Sage, answered King Calid's question as to the matter of the Stone in the following way : " It is of thee, O King, and thou art its ore." And Raymond asserted that he had extracted his substance from a vile and worthless thing. Yet you are not to suppose that I would

take any kind of Mercury for this purpose without exercising any discrimi-
nation; rather, like a wise carpenter,
I would pass over the green and
unseasoned timber, and select for my
structure only that which is seasoned
and dry. Common Mercury, and
animal and vegetable Mercury, might
be used for our purpose; but the labour
of preparing and digesting it would be
very great. And even if you could get
it easily, it would be comparatively
useless. For you cannot be sure of a
flame where there are only a few feeble
sparks; and only vigorous and exuberant Mercury is really suitable for our
purpose — epithets which are by no
means applicable to the feeble Mercury
of vegetables and animals. We have
to take into consideration the fact that
the Mercury must be fixed by means of
its own inherent sulphur, acted on by
external heat. This heat proceeds from
the heavenly bodies, and the form will
be different according to the description
of the heavenly body by which the

Mercury is set in motion. Bodies receive their figure, lineaments, and temper from water, their fixation from the dryness of the earth, and are more or less matured according to the velocity or slowness of the inward fire. If Saturn governs this motion, and there is an aqueous surface, we get lead; if Jupiter be lord of the motion, tin is produced; where Mars predominates, we get iron. The Sun is thus the cause of gold, Venus of copper, the Moon of silver. Quicksilver is produced by Mercury, which is more or less good or bad according to the perfect character of the motion. It is thus, then, that we must think of the metals, if we would profoundly enter into their nature. Our object in this Art is to change metals into gold and silver; but as gold and silver are malleable, and have their own proper qualities and colours, the seeds of all these things must be in the substance, or else they can never be brought to maturity. Hence we may exclude from our search not only ani-

mals and vegetables, but common
Mercury, marcasite, and all lesser
minerals. For none of these contain
a Mercury suitable for our purpose,
seeing that we need a Mercury in which
is inherent its own principle of fixation
and animation. It is true that the
heavenly bodies are efficient causes of
all things, and consequently also of
marcasite, etc. ; nevertheless, the mar-
casites, pyrites, and similar minerals,
differ greatly from metallic substances
in the arrangement of these principles.
For they are quickened by simple Mercury, and the direct influence of some
heavenly body. But the other minerals,
though they too are set in motion by
simple Mercury, receive the influence of
two or three, or even more heavenly
luminaries of different complexion and
character, by the confusion of which
these bodies are affected in contradictory
ways, and are regarded as imperfect in
respect of our magistery. But the
question might arise in regard to the
inferior metals, how they can contain the

principle of gold and silver, seeing that, to the vulgar eye, they would seem to have nothing in common with those metals, and least of all with gold. We answer that the end of our Art requires two things, fixed earth and mineral water, which exist in all metals, though after a diverse manner, in some actually, and in others at least potentially, but really and essentially in all. It is indeed true that everything depends on the influence of heavenly bodies. But no one substance is predestined to be acted on by any one heavenly body, and if a metal which has been under the influence of Mars, should come under the influence of the Sun, it will gradually exhibit corresponding changes. If the motive power be twofold, twofold effects will be traceable in the metallic subject. Saturn is, in respect of Aquarius, cold and dry; in respect of Capricorn, hot and dry; hotness and coldness will contend for the mastery, and warmth will occupy the centre. Similarly, Sagittarius is near Mars, Aries near Jupiter,

Taurus near Venus, Virgo near Mercury, which all agree in heat, and are therefore the same in the subject metals. However different they may be in height and depth, they will agree in width. For Saturn is hot within, cold without, while dryness is contiguous to both. It is after a like fashion with Mercury and Venus. The extremes of Jupiter are bound together by humidity; and it is the same with Mars. Thus the first three inferior metals belong to the same terrestrial, and the last two to the same aquatic, latitude. The surface of Saturn is held by Aquarius, of Jupiter by Pisces, of Mars by Scorpio, of Venus by Libra, of Mercury by Gemini, which are reputed frigid signs; hence the said bodies agree in longitude as well as in latitude. Again, as hot bodies are variously digested according as they are dry or moist, so cold bodies are variously affected in their passivity, and this is the reason why metallic bodies of common latitudes differ so greatly in their forms. Venus and Jupiter are in the same longitude of coldness, but differ a whole hemisphere in their passive elements, since the coldness of Jupiter is accompanied with moisture, while that of Venus coexists with dryness, the form of the one depending on water, of the other on earth. So Venus and Saturn agree in longitude, latitude, and depth, but differ in form, because the latitude of Venus is dominated by fire, that of Saturn by earth. In the same way, gold and silver receive their forms from their own proper motive forces; the former is begotten of a single parent, the Sun, cherishing the Lion within and without, hot and moist, cold and dry, evenly tempered throughout. For being furnished with fixation within, it possesses the maturing force of fire in every atom, and this maturity is perfect life. Further, this maturity is the result of a long development, for no gold is generated suddenly in its ore, but out of its own seed and first principle, which we call fire, acting on Mercury in every part. Now I say that this seed, this principle, this elemental fire, this first substance exists in all inferior metals, though in different degrees of development. Hence all these inferior metals in their inner being are potentially gold, and do potentially possess metallic life ; and there is no difference between gold and these inferior metals, except in degree of maturity. The mineral water and earth may thus by proper digestion be brought to the perfection and excellence of gold, if the heavenly rays, which are instrumental in the ripening of that metal, can be brought to bear on them. In regard to this matter different Sages have written in such different ways that it is not easy to reconcile their statements. What one affirms to be good and convenient is uncompromisingly rejected by another, so that any one who strives to gain a knowledge of this Art by reading and comparing books must be fairly puzzled. Hence there have been very few that have ever been rightly and adequately acquainted with this secret; for not every one who knows the matter,

and is cognisant in a mechanical way of
the method of preparing it, is deserving
of the name of a Sage. For he may
know nothing of the theory of physics,
or the *rationale* of our Art, or of the
causes why the nature of gold is imparted to other metals. But, as the poet
has it,

Blessed is he who knows the gods of the fields,
And Pan, and aged Sylvanus, and the sister
nymphs.

Men who have a mere practical knowledge of Alchemy know how
to make gold, but the same are not
Sages. They cling desperately to
the particular method which they have
been taught, and decry everything else
as false and unscientific, since they do
not know the universality of the substance, nor the different ways of manipu-
lating it They think their one little
branch is the whole tree of Philosophy,
and thus have obscured the entire garden
of the Hesperides with the fumes of their
ignorance. There is another class of
men, whom I call rationalists, or dog-

matists, who have reduced the universal science to rules, and have laid down codes of weight, quantity, time, etc., as of general application, though they apply only to particular cases. The third class are the Methodists, who base the principle of their teaching on that which, to others, is the end of the Magistery. They differ from the Rationalists in that they veil in simple and every-day language the most momentous mysteries of our Stone. They say that silver and gold are quickened Mercury, and that they consist of water and earth (including the other elements), and have spoken only of Mercury without any specific restrictions. They say also that out of either of the said bodies the same thing can be prepared, viz., a Stone producing exactly similar effects. Saturn, for instance, which consists of water and earth, may be taken as the ore of the substance: the water may be changed into earth, and thus into our red, fixed powder, which, after fermentation, becomes our Stone. This method the

ancient Sages have called the Royal
Way. Another, more subtle, method is
that by which Saturn is dissolved by
water, or the vegetable menstruum, into
the four elements, which are then purified, re-united, and, by calcination and
fermentation, become the Stone. The
third way is to change Saturn into our
mineral water, or to join this quicksilver
of Saturn to that of gold, and let it
receive the colour or tincture of gold.
The methods will be different in dealing
with Mercury gained from Mars, Jupiter,
and Venus. From gold it can be obtained
in at least twenty-seven different ways,
which the ancient Sages called the
mansions of the Moon. For as the
Moon passes through all the signs in
twenty-seven days, or at most in thirty,
so the mineral water of the Sages, placed
in these twenty-seven positions, runs
through the whole metallic firmament,
and assumes the properties of all the
inferior metals. He that would accom-
plish this Magistery successfully should
know the conformation of all metals, and

the heavenly influences by which all
earthly things are generated, moved, and
disposed.   He must also understand the
harmony and mutual relations of active
and passive elements, and how to judge
of them by outward phenomena; further,
he must know also how to unite extremes by means of their common
qualities.   For as no building can be
perfect the idea of which was not first
completely conceived in the mind of the
architect, so you cannot know what to
do in dealing with these inferior metals
unless you have an exact acquaintance
with all the conditions of the work.
How, for instance, can he be said to
know more of silver than a mere clown
who does not understand the influence
of the Moon in producing its form, the
sphere in which it revolves, the rate of
its velocity, the causes of its numerous
apparent irregularities, of its shifting
position with regard to the Sun and the
Earth, of its eclipses, and so on.   For
every difference in the heavens must
produce a corresponding modification on

earth. Do not wandering stars, when they sometimes go forward, then backwards, then stop for a time, produce a corresponding effect on earth? We have also to reckon with the movements of the planets, their changing relative positions, their deflexions, sometimes towards the south, and then again towards the north; none of these can be unattended with results here below. For every celestial movement is the cause of a terrestrial effect. The Sage must also be greatly helped by a knowledge of the occultations and reappearances of the planets, and their certain and irrefragable causes. For thereby the eyes of the mind are opened, and we look deep into the mysteries of Nature, the causes of dissolution and composition, of heat and cold; the cloud of mystery is lifted in which all sublunar bodies move, and assume this or that form. Without a profound insight into these things you can have no real knowledge of our Art; while, on the other hand, such knowledge is the mother of practical skill. With

this information there can be no difficulty
in tracing all the steps which lie between
the finding of the matter and the perfection of the Stone; for these steps are
not the arbitrary suggestions of chance,
but the natural and necessary development of the genus inherent in the first
matter. You know the beginning and
the end; the intermediate part of our
Magistery cannot fail to be suggested to
you by your acquaintance with physical
processes. There are water and mineral
earth united in the same substance; into
this you are to introduce the form of
gold, consisting also of mineral water
and fixed earth. Can you doubt how
you are to develop the exuberant qualities of the substance ? Nothing can be
introduced into this mineral water and
earth except what belongs to the same
genus. The development is brought
about by one inward agent, without
which not so much as the name of our
Art would ever have been heard of.
This agent is sought by many, but found
by few. It is a precious liquid which

does not tender its services to the multitude, but is the handmaiden of Sages. Some think it is common Mercury exposed to violent heat in a glass vessel; others say the Mercury must be very gently distilled in a glass vessel and rarefied. But all these persons are ignorant philosophasters. Raymond indeed describes a similar process, but he means something quite different, viz., that our Mercury is to be purified in a brilliant vessel, not to elicit water from it, but to free it by fire from its crudity, and to make it more readily soluble. Other methods, like the one suggested by the monk Ravilascius, not only betray gross ignorance, but are altogether absurd. Neither in one way nor the other can our water be elicited from common Mercury, or the mysteries of our Magistery be unlocked. There is no menstruum which can so dissolve this Mercury that it shall retain its form; yet that is what our Art requires. Moreover, it seems absurd that the greater should be dominated by the less.

For instance, the Moon is passive with
regard to the Planets, and yet is said to
act on every one of those which are
placed beneath it. Should Mercury,
then, which contains within itself the
sphere of the Moon, be affected by the
Moon? No; and much less can higher
bodies be affected by Mercury, seeing
that Mercury is rather affected by them.
Even if common Mercury could be dissolved, it could exercise its power only
on the Moon which is contiguous to it.
If we follow reason, it will tell us that
the greater contains the less, and that
this common Mercury has hitherto been
accounted a slave and not a master.
Saturn, on the other hand, includes
within its circle the spheres of all the
rest; by its virtue lead is produced, and
it also has caused that metallic water to
contain within it all essential properties.
For not only can the Stone be prepared
from lead, as we have shewn, but lead
itself may become the Stone. Its water
will be a menstruum to all the rest, nor
will the same thing that will dissolve

lead dissolve the rest, as we will explain
presently. As it is the property of this
menstruum to dissolve, we will speak of
it now.

Solution is the action of any body,
which, by certain laws of innate sympathy, assimilates anything of a lower
class to its own essence. But among
metals there is no form more vigorous
or powerful than that of Saturn, and
therefore the solvent of Saturn must be
sought in the vegetable world. This
vegetable must agree with Saturn in its
properties. Now among minerals Saturn
is furthest removed from maturity, and
therefore our vegetable substance must
also be highly immature. As sweetness
is distinctive of maturity, so sourness
attends on immaturity, which, moreover,
is the result of cold, while maturity is of
heat. Our menstruum, or solvent, then,
must be a sour vegetable water. Moreover, as lead is crude at the centre and
pure near the circumference, the vegetable menstruum which Nature has in-
vented for dissolving lead, must be of

the same kind. There are two other solvents which have all the characteristics of gold and silver, being fixed bodies of sensitive temperament, and possessing the power of dissolving these metals, because they are quite free from all crudity; and the one solvent which is gold the Ancients have called the greater menstruum. The menstruum of Saturn they call the smaller, because it has no power over gold. Only gold and silver possess the quality of dissolving themselves, because there is no metal above them to exercise that power. Gold can also dissolve copper and quicksilver, though it is not true that common Mercury absorbs gold, which is no more possible than that the sphere of Mercury should include the sphere in which the Sun itself moves. The Greater Menstruum, or water of Mercury, as some call it, though it dissolves gold and silver, produces a more complete and rapid effect in the case of tin. Mars is contiguous to the Sun, and, being of noble quality, harmonizes more with the

Sun and Moon, and by virtue of its position is called the proper and perfect instrument for moving the Sun. Those who would dissolve the Sun must dissolve Jupiter through Saturn into the water of Mars, afterwards with the lymph of Jupiter, and gold with the menstruum of Mars, for thus the virtues of our substance will conveniently be exercised. Furthermore, the Sun, by means of its moisture, dissolves Venus, by the dew of which common Mercury may be rendered liquid. This liquid at length will dissolve the Moon. But it must not be supposed that remote bodies, like Jupiter and Saturn, can dissolve others through their own proper immediate virtues. We have, indeed, defined dissolution as a certain action whereby, in accordance with the laws of Sympathy, one body assimilates and elevates others to its own virtue, but this is to be understood only of contiguous bodies. Saturn, which embraces the sphere of Jupiter, is subjected to Mars, and Mars, again, through the mediation of Jupiter, acts on Saturn. But as the nature of Mars is most fitted to dissolve the Sun, Saturn, which has the same properties, may do the same, not, however, by virtue of its own proper nature, but because the nature of Mars is included in that of Saturn. This is to be understood of all the rest, after their kind. Hitherto we have explained the art of dissolving metallic bodies, by means of their own threefold menstruum, into their proximate principles, viz., water and earth. Now, we will briefly describe the method of reducing metals into a more remote substance, viz., quicksilver. I will here take no notice of the venomous sayings of malicious astrologers ; I shall have a word to address to them presently, when I shall also treat of the conjunctions and diameters of the planets, with their periodic and real syzigiæ. Take Venus, or copper, the subject on which you desire to operate, and remember that you are trying to render visible a part which in its very nature is close to the centre. Ask

under what sign of the horoscope Venus
rises, and you will find that it is under the
sign of Taurus in the fifteenth degree,
at a right angle to the rising Sun ; turn
your eyes to the west, and you will see
the Scorpion in the same degree, before
which is the surface of Mars, naturally
cold and dry, directed toward the earth.
Note these things down. In the third
point of the sky and in the tenth house,
you will find the Lion. Now, the Lion
is the animal of the Sun, which you
need under the given angles as an intermediate substance. Follow the guidance,
and imitate these heavenly relations in
your terrestrial astronomy, *i.e.*, take the
menstrual water of gold, purify twice or
thrice from the earth, or the calx of iron,
pour drop by drop on the body of Venus,
which has first been melted, and it will
in a few moments become liquid Mercury, as our Art requires. Take the
water of lead stiffened with the earth of
iron (Mars), to dissolve the Sun, and so
with the rest. Moreover, the Sun, according to this rule, while the Lion

ascends will be opposite Saturn in
Aquarius, whose surface imitates the
nature of water; in their middle, as it
were, or in the middle of Heaven, will
be the Tabernacle and House of Mars.
In this way every mineral is reduced to
the nature of its second component part.
But do not say too much, Kelly; for
already smoke ascends in the distance
from the roofs of the houses, and the
shadows of the hills begin to lengthen.

## How to Prepare the Stone with Water and Earth.

WHEN the gum distils in the right way, remove the vessel containing the earth from the fire, as soon as all the water that we call menstruum has evaporated. Then break the vessel a little above the clay which covers the bottom part. In this way the black earth will be kindled of its own accord, and calcine itself marvellously—a secret which the Sages would not commit to writing; they only said that our Stone could calcine, cleanse, dissolve, multiply, and perfect itself. While the earth is kindled like a live coal, it should be stirred with an iron rod, so that all its parts may be perfectly calcined. Then take a fine sieve, finer than the earth, as soon as it has become cold, and purify it from the crumbs of Saturn. Place in the egg of the Sages, add the water, at first with-

out any distillation, and immediately
seal up the egg hermetically. In this
way all the water will be absorbed by
its earth. This is the great secret, of
which the Sages say that the hour of
the birth of the infant, *i.e.*, water, must
not be permitted, but joined at once
with its own milk, *i.e.*, the ferment.
This is the dragon that devours its own
tail, or the serpents in the Saliatic
whirlpool, of which one has wings (*i.e.*,
water), while the other, earth, has no
wings. This is that divine stone which
is of itself, is prepared in itself, tinges
itself, and ferments and multiplies itself.
This is that work which if a man understand the same, he must not divulge to
his brother. Place the rest, with closed
mouth, in the athanor, digest gradually,
for it has passed through all changes
and colours. Consider the noble bird,
*i.e.*, the infant. This bird is a man
born when the Sun was in Aries, *i.e.*, in
March, whose tunic must be cut off by
the nurse, and this also is the man of
March. In selecting it, consider that it

must be taken out of its uncorrupted
ore, *i.e.*, out of the woman and the man,
and buried not only in the earth, but in
a dung heap, and the common streets;
for, as the Sages say, it is buried in the
streets. This, says the Sage, is the
thing which all have, and yet there is no
greater secret under heaven, by which
diseases are cured, metals transmuted,
and all things accomplished. It passes
through so many admirable colours that
they cannot be described. It is dis
solved into water in three days in the
athanor. It is the perfect minera of
white and red sulphur in animals, and
we have once seen it cause teeth to
grow in the mouth of an old man.
Ripley affirms of this wonderful Stone:
Remember that man is the noblest
creature on earth, in whom is a neutral
Mercuriality of the four elements pro-
portioned by Nature; for our two
metals are nothing but the brilliant ores
of our Sun and our lucid Moon, as
Raymundus wisely notes. The method
is as follows: Make first the Mercurial

water of the Moon, that is to say, take
aqua fortis made in the ordinary way of
salt and vitriol, rectify three or four times,
for every such water without frequent
rectification is useless; dissolve in this
water two ounces of pure Moon, and
digest the solution twenty days in a
pelican vessel. Place in retort, and
drive off aqua fortis in the bath. Repeat till the water comes forth like
spring water. Add fresh water, and
repeat the former operation, that the
silver may be calcined by the fire while
its humidity, contrary to Nature, is preserved and even augmented. Remove
all water, collect that which is dissolved
by the violent steam of the bath, and
dissolve in five ounces of our white
menstrual water. Circulate for a month,
cleanse of its sediment, distil menstruum,
and there will remain the Oil of the
Moon. If it be not yet perfectly clear,
add more menstrual water, till it become
perfectly liquid and pure. This is called
our menstrual water of the Moon. In
the same way dissolve an ounce of

gold in the Royal water, made through rectification of aqua fortis with burnt Sun, digest for twenty days, then often separate, and add the water, until it shall have become thin; then well liquefy the Sol with fresh water so that it flows like wax; then take four ounces of our oil or menstruum, and dissolve the said gold, afterwards triturating in a well-closed glass vessel for 20 days; dissolve repeatedly. Then the gold will be well purified, and this is the male and female substance, which must be united in this work with water of Antimony. Distil the King or Regulus of Antimony and sub-limed Mercury in the ordinary way, till it becomes a viscous water, which must be rectified of its sediment twice in a hot bath, or by pouring it seven times through sand. Take three parts of this water, two parts of the water of the Moon, one part of Sol, and place in our philoso-phical egg, so that it is one-third full. Digest by twofold circulation, as you know, and it will become the true Magis-tery for transmuting Mercury into gold.

## An Easy Way of Making the Tincture.

-----

TAKE one ounce of gold, dissolve in Royal Water, steam off all aqua fortis by heat of ashes or sand, pour on this substance a good part of Spirit of Saturn, and it will immediately receive a deep colouring. Place the whole solution in retort, and steam off spirit with gentle heat. Pour this solution over the gold, as before, remove after two hours, and separate by gentle heat from the solution. The spirit is thus intensified and illuminated with the rays of the sun. The gold may then be melted and used for ordinary purposes, as it is not further serviceable in this work. Place spirit in pelican, with one ounce of common Mercury seven times sublimed, seal up hermetically with best wax, and place in steam bath at a moderate heat; after five or six weeks the Mercury will begin to dissolve, and, wonderful to relate, will be sublimed on the surface of the water, which is tinged with a black and reddish colour, and this quintessence is afterwards coagulated with the Mercury into a snow white powder. Finally, let the vessel be placed in an athanor with a head or cover, fashioned in the form of a pelican, wherein the substance is digested into a yellow, and afterwards into a black, powder.

## A Way of Making Potable Gold.

THERE are two kinds of potable gold. One is called Elixir, and is the stone liquefied into oil; the other is extracted from melted calx of gold with the red oil of Saturn. All other recipes and methods of alchemists are inept and far from our intention, for whatsoever is reduced into a body, the same is crude and undecocted. Nature develops what is good into what is better by the way of alteration. Gold which has not passed through alteration or physical solution has not been educed into something better. Take oil of lead, and circulate for forty days in a steam bath. Distil in retort till more than half has ascended, and then there will be seen in the vessel a white and crystalline water remaining at the bottom, while the oil floats on the surface. Take up this oil, and place the

water by itself, as it is worthless; distil
this oil slowly two or three times; when
quite free from water, circulate for three
days, then rectify, and it will be ready.
Take one ounce of common purified
gold, amalgamate with twelve parts of
Mercury twice sublimed and revivified.
Distil Mercury, and the gold will remain
as a fine powder. This powder place
with calx of gold in pelican, pour on it
the aforesaid oil, digest for twelve days.
Pour the solution into a transparent and
flat retort, free from all grit and sediment, steam off the oil in a lukewarm
bath, till a thick golden gum remains at
the bottom; dry the gold, calcine in a dry
fire, and dissolve with the oil as before.
The gum which results is potable and
no longer reducible into a body. There
is no other method under heaven of
physically dissolving the body of gold,
and concerning it Ripley, a man and a
philosopher who is honourable for all
eternity, writes as follows:—

" The nature of the Sun being
most pure enriches the air, mixes

and matures it, puts to flight the plague, nourishes and purifies the air, sweetens roses, dries up noxious humours, softens and hardens and cleanses Nature. It causes all things to grow, and replaces drought with verdure. It is verdant in laurel, and laughs brightly in gold, generates stones, and calls into life gleaming bodies."

Dissolve purified gold in distilled vinegar; dissolve for three days, then pass through filter, and evaporate till it is thick and becomes a gum, of which you must have 24 pounds; put three into a vessel, and distil with gentle heat in sand; when it is not moved by the fire add coals; thus elicit the humidity gradually and skilfully, till you see a white vapour ascend into the alembic. Take a large receiver, tie it up with cloth, and put in cold water. Keep up a gentle and equable fire, so that the spirits may not enter the receiver more quickly than they can be dissolved, which would cause the vessel to burst, and would not be without danger to the artist. If the drops flow too slowly, increase the fire a little, and towards the end you want a fierce fire; so do not save your coals then. When you have so collected all the moisture from the 24 pounds, circulate it twice in a pelican over a gentle fire. Then take a tall vessel, distil slowly, till a water comes out which burns like spirit of wine. Keep this, and pour the remainder into a large and tall retort, and place in balneum till you see how, by means of the distillation an oil is separated (its phlegm still remaining in the retort) and floats on the surface. This oil skim off, for it is the Oil of Mercury, in which the Sun can be dissolved. Subtilize the said oil in the pelican over a gentle fire, then rectify once and again. This is the preparation of the true mercurial water, or the female. Now comes the preparation of the male, or the gold. Transfer the pure, unmixed body of gold into Mercury, either according to the common philosophical way, or according to that

of *terra damnata*, stirring with the tool
Trycsitrock for an hour. The first
method is performed as follows :—Take
menstruum of Saturn, and add calcined
Jupiter in an iron spoon : strain, reduce
to powder, and dissolve with the menstruum of Saturn; rectify once and
again, and add thin crocus (sulphur) of
Mars. The tepid bath will melt it into
a reddish water; purge off the menstruum till red drops fall down; change
receiver, drive off the reddish liquid of
Mars, and rectify it again and again. The
virtue of the solvent well be then intensified. Take black earth of lead, to wit,
of your minium, which remains at the
bottom of the vessel after the extraction
of the water of life, or spirit of Saturn,
and if you calcine it for a couple of hours,
it becomes yellow ; pour on this the prepared water of Mars, and distil once and
again ; in this way it will be strengthened. At this point you should have
ready finely pulverised gold, to which
apply the fortified menstruum of Mars,
and the tepid heat of the bath, and it will

then be reduced in a few moments to
Mercury. Put eight ounces of this
Mercury into a glass vessel, of which it
should fill the eighth part. Place in a
low furnace, filled with sand, and increase the heat week by week, and it
will be precipitated in forty days. This
is the preparation of your gold: now
comes its fermentation. Have in readi-
ness an oval vessel, the third part of
which holds eight ounces of the said oil
of Saturn; add two ounces of your
precipitated gold; seal up the vessel,
place on athanor, when the gold will be
absorbed and dissolved in a few hours.
After the forty days it will begin to grow
black, and our gentle heat will carry it
through all the stages of blackness.
Increase the heat, and you will behold,
successively, all the different shades of
white; then it will become yellow, and
finally, a deep red colour; remove the
black earth, called *terra damnata*, which
after 24 hours fierce heat will be found
at the bottom of the vessel, and your
tincture is ready; the same will in-

stantly reduce all metals to Mercury. Remove the surface crudity of this Mercury by stirring it with Trycsitrock.

The way of multiplying the tincture is as follows :—Take equal parts of Oil of Saturn and dissolved Stone, in which you have previously dissolved gold ; digest in a closed vessel, and the first time it will be perfected in six months, the second time in three months ; the third time, it will pass through all the colours in one month ; the fourth time in two weeks ; the fifth time in a week ; the sixth time in three days. Then it is too subtle to be multiplied any more, but you must begin afresh.

END OF KELLY'S TRACT.

# The Secret of the
## Four Waters of Perfection.

VITRIOL 3 lb., alum (purified) 2 lb., saltpetre 1 lb. From these you obtain, with aqua fortis, the simple water of the first degree. For the second water of perfection take 1 lb. of the first water, and dissolve in it 4 oz. of salt armoniac; this water then assumes another colour, it dissolves the Sun, and constitutes the second water of perfection. For the third water take 20 oz. of the aforesaid water, with 8 oz. of sublimed, well pounded Mercury; mix, seal up, plunge in hot ashes; when the Mercury is dissolved, it is the third water of perfection, and when it is poured on a plate of copper, the same receives the colour of silver. This water burns with a white and fetid flame, against which you must be on your guard. For the fourth water, take of this water and sublimed Mercury, plunge in sealed vessel, in horsedung, for a fortnight, and it will assume an imperfect blue and a yellowish colour; distil living water, through ashes, over a gentle fire, and you have the virgin's milk. The first water dissolves. the Moon, calcines Mercury, blackens the skin, and is of the first degree. The second water dissolves gold and Mercury, sublimes sulphur, stains the skin orange, and is of the second degree. The third water changes copper into the colour of silver, and reduces all metals to their first matter. The fourth water reduces all calcined, pulverised bodies to the first matter. and is called the clear and living water; it is also heavy, and is called the virgin's milk; it is sharp, strong, and bitter; if one drop falls on copper it perforates it, and it forms white crystals when it is distilled like other waters. This water in distillation and putre-faction is free from all the corrosiveness of sulphur, and dissolves metals into their first matter instead of corroding them; it is cleansed from all sediment, and impurity, and hardness of iron, of which all metals, even copper, retain a trace, and which is blue in colour. Take any calcined metallic filings, mix with salt pounded small, wash with hot salt water, dry, cover this powder to the height of two inches with oil of tartar, seal up, plunge in horsedung for eight days so that it may putrefy. Take it out of the vessel, pour off the oil, dry the powder slowly in warm ashes, put into living water (our fourth water), let the vessel be subjected to heat, and you will see how the powder melts into Mercury. Carefully empty the water into another vessel, and there will remain the new Mercury, which is corporeal, and not volatile like other Mercury; wash with hot water and common salt, and dry. Strain through a cloth; if any amalgam remains on the cloth, put it once more into the living water, till it becomes quick Mercury; repeat this till all the Mercury has passed through the cloth. This is our magisterial, corporeal Mercury of signal perfection, and not the common kind. Its signs are these: that in its running it is not like simple Mercury; that when placed on a body which is not fixed in the fire, so far as it spreads over that body it fixes it. Thus it fixes all bodies which were not fixed before, and in the above way you can get as much corporeal Mercury as you like. If you have made 20 oz. of this Mercury, take 5⅓ oz. of filings, pound small, add 10⅔ oz. of corporeal Mercury, form an amalgam by pounding (making a soft paste). Divide amalgam into three parts, put into vessel, take one part of calcined body, and three parts of corporeal Mercury, mix well, add to other two parts of amalgam, mix well, let it stand in the vessel in hot ashes till the whole substance is changed into Mercury, and thus you can multiply this Mercury infinitely, so long as you have metal filings of any kind.

# The Theatre

## OF

# Terrestrial Astronomy.

# THE THEATRE OF TERRESTRIAL ASTRONOMY.

MANY books have been written on the art of Alchemy, which, by the multiplicity of their allegories, riddles, and parables, bewilder and confound all earnest students; and the cause of this confusion is the vast number and variety of names, which all signify and do set forth one and the same thing. For this reason I have resolved in my own mind to loosen and untie all the difficult knots of the ancient Sages. I will speak first of the inventors and restorers of this Art; secondly, of the mutual conversion of elements, and how through the predominance of one element the substance of metals is generated; thirdly, I will shew the affinity and homogeneity of metals, procreated in the bowels of

the earth, their sympathies and anti-
pathies, according to the purity and
impurity of their Sulphur and Mercury ;
and that as metals consist of Sulphur
and Mercury, they can furnish us with
the first matter of the Elixir; 4°, the
preparation of Mercurial water; 5°, the
conversion of prepared Mercury into
Mercurial earth ; 6°, the exaltation of
Mercurial water; 7°, the solution of gold
by Mercurial water; 8°, the preparation
of the water or Moon of the Sages; 9°,
the conjunction of sun and moon ; 10°,
the blackness, or Raven's Head, by
means of which the solution and copulation of Sun and Moon do both take
place; 11°, the peacock's tail ; 12°, the
white Tincture ; 13°, the perfect red
Elixir. This Art being given by Divine
inspiration, and as a secret revealed
from above, we implore God's help for
every part of our work, the small as well
as the great, for He alone hath the
power to give or to withhold this knowledge from whomsoever He will. No
one taketh this honour to himself, but

God alone can enlighten the eyes and lift the cloud of natural mysteries, so that albeit you cannot understand the plainest things without Him, yet will you apprehend the most difficult arcana if He give you light. I will now speak of the illustrious men who, before and after the Flood, have discovered and established the chemical Art.

## Chapter the First.

### Of the Inventors and Restorers of this Art.

ALL Sages agree that the knowledge of this Art was first imparted to Adam by the Holy Spirit, and He prophesied, both before and after the Fall, that the world must be renewed, or, rather, purged with water. Therefore his successors erected two stone tables, on which they engraved a summary of all physical arts, in order that this arcanum might become known to posterity. After the Flood, Noah found one of these tables at the foot of Mount Ararat. Others say that the knowledge of the Art was restored by Hermes Trismegistus, whose mind was a treasury of all arts and sciences; and alchemists are still called sons of Hermes. Bernard of Trevisa states that the said Hermes came to the valley of Hebron, and there found seven stone tables, on which a summary of the seven liberal Arts had been inscribed before the Flood; for this same Hermes flourished both before and after the Flood, and is identified with Noah. Then this Art found its way into Persia, Egypt, and Chaldæa. The Hebrews called it the Cabbala, the Persians Magia, and the Egyptians Sophia, and it was taught in the schools together with Theology; it was known to Moses, Abraham, Solomon, and the Magi who came to Christ from the East. Magia derived its origin from the doctrine of the Divine Ternary and the Trinity of God. For God has stamped and sealed all created things with this character of Trinity, as a kind of hieroglyphical writing, whereby His own nature might be known. For the number 3 and the magic number 4 make up the perfect number 7, the seat of many mysteries. And seeing that the Quaternary rests in the Ternary, it is a number which stands on the horizon of eternity, and doth exhibit everything bound with God in us, thus including

God, men, and all created things, with all their mysterious powers. Adding three, you get ten, which marks the return to unity. In this arcanum is concluded all knowledge of hidden things which God, by His word, has made known to the men of His good pleasure, so that they might have a true conception of Him. And this is the figure which is called the sphere of Heaven. The said sphere consists of a circle, which circle represents the

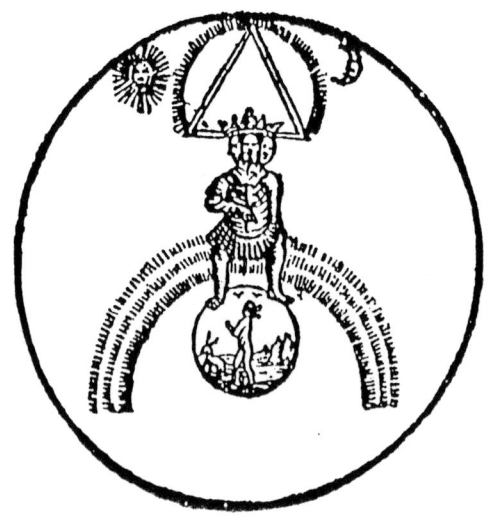

Trinity of the Deity in unity, God with three heads and one crown, surmounted

by a triangle, encircled with a rainbow, and above the sun and moon. The first colour of the rainbow, on which God sits, is black, with the sign of Saturn ; the second, dark brown, with the sign of Jupiter; the third, red, with the sign of Mars ; the fourth, green and yellow, with the sign of the Sun ; the fifth, green, with the sign of Venus; the sixth, yellow, green, white, and red, with the sign of Mercury ; the seventh, a silver grey, with the sign of the Moon, and yellow beneath.

His feet are placed on the terrestrial globe, in which are animals and hills, with a white and brown man, whose eyes are bandaged, and an egg is between his feet.

---

## CHAPTER THE SECOND.

### *Of the Mutual Conversion of Elements ; how one element predominates over another ; whence the substance of the metals is generated.*

Geber, Morienus, and other Sages have pronounced the conversion of one

element into another a very necessary
process in the composition of the Stone :
convert the elements, and you have what
you seek.   There are four elements, air,
water, fire, earth, with their four qualities, hot, cold, moist, dry.   Two are
active, air and fire, and two passive,
water and earth.   Two are light, and
two heavy.   Contradictory qualities are
united only by means of a third.   Hot
and dry are not contradictory, and
therefore form the element of air; cold
and dry are not contradictory, and
become earth;   nor are cold and moist,
which constitute water :   but hot and
cold are united only by means of a
medium, viz., dry, as otherwise they
would destroy each other.   Hence hot
and cold are united and separated by
dissolving and coagulating the homogeneous quality.   Moist and dry, on the
other hand, are united and separated by
constriction and humectation ; simple
generation and natural transmutation
are by the operation of the elements.
For those elements which conquer cold

generate that which is hot. It is clear
that all things are generated by heat and
cold ; and all elements must belong to the
same genus, or else they could not act on
each other. After creating the matter
of the metals, namely, living Mercury,
Nature added to it an active quality.
For Mercury, the substance, could not
of itself manifest its effects, and Nature
wisely joined to it an active kind of
mineral earth, unctuous and fat, thickened by long digestion in the mineral
caverns of the earth, which is commonly
called Sulphur. This Mercury is, however, not the common metal, but the
principle and origin of metals. Mercury is the matter, Sulphur the form of
metals, natural heat acting on the matter
of Mercury, as upon a fit and well
adapted subject.

The picture represents a black rock,
on the summit of which stand black
Saturn ; Jupiter, the white king ; Mars,
the red soldier ; Sol, with a golden head
and ruddy neck ; Venus, in a green
robe ; Mercury, with helmet, and red,

green, purple, white, yellow, ochre, black
gown, and yellow, red, blue wings ; the
Moon white and black.

On the black plain stands Mercury
of many colours, the Moon with the sign
⌣ on her head, and Sulphur on both
sides of Mercury is signified by the term
Hermaphrodite ; the four elements from
the four corners blow upon the place
where Mercury and the Moon are.

CHAPTER THE THIRD.

*Of the Homogeneous Affinity of Metals
generated in the bowels of the Earth;
Harmony and Antipathy of Metallic
Qualities.
Metals consist of Mercury and Sulphur,
and furnish us with the first substance
of the Elixir.*

The various conversions of the
elements which produce the first matter
of metals have been now described.
We must next treat of the nature of the
said metals. It is clearer than daylight
that there are seven planets, seven days,
seven metals, and seven operations.
The metals are called after the planets,
because of their influence and their
mutual relations. The mineral principles are living Mercury and Sulphur.
From these are generated all metals and
minerals, of which there are many
species, possessing diverse natures, according to the purity and impurity of the
Mercury and Sulphur, resulting in the
purity or impurity of the generated

metal. Gold is a perfect body, of pure, clear, red Mercury, and pure, fixed, red, incombustible Sulphur. Silver is a pure body, nearly approaching perfection, of pure, clear, fixed white Mercury, and Sulphur of the same kind ; it is a little wanting in fixation, colour, and weight. Tin is a pure, imperfect body, of pure, fixed and unfixed, clear, white Mercury outside, and red Mercury inside, with Sulphur of the same kind. Lead is an impure, imperfect body, of impure, unfixed, earthy, white, fetid Mercury and Sulphur outside, and red Mercury inside, with Sulphur of the same quality. Copper is an impure and imperfect body, of impure, unfixed, dirty, combustible, red Sulphur and Mercury. It is deficient in fixation, purity, and weight, while it abounds in impure colour and combustible terrestreity. Iron is of impure, imperfect, excessively fixed, earthy, burning, white and red Sulphur and Mercury, is wanting in fusion, purity, and weight, abounding in fixed, impure Sulphur and combustible terrestreity.

Nature transmutes the elements into
Mercury, just as Sulphur transmutes the
first matter. The nature of all metals
must be the same, because their first
substance is the same, and Nature cannot develop anything out of a substance
that is not in it.

The picture represents a black
rock, on which stand, hand in hand, the
planets : 1, Black Saturn, falling down ;
2, Jupiter ; 3, Mars ; 4, Mercury of many
colours ; 5, Venus, with green robe, and
the Sun and Moon. Lower down, on
the black rock, stands an old man with

a pick-axe, cutting a piece out of the
rock, whence Saturn falls, and near
him lie, as if dead, Jupiter and Saturn.

---

### Chapter the Fourth.

*Of the Preparation of Mercurial Earth.*

Know that out of all metals a
perfect Medicine can be made, which
can transmute the remaining metals into
gold and silver ; for out of the perfect

metals you get, by proper separation of
elements, the Salt of Nature, otherwise
Ore of the Philosophers, by some called

Philosophical Lili, without which the work of the Sages cannot be accomplished. For Art presupposes a substance created by Nature alone, in which Art assists Nature and Nature assists Art.

A vessel like an urinal stands, encircled at its base by a ring of twisted straw; within it are Mercury, Mars, and Saturn, lying on their backs, and an old man is on the point of throwing in Venus and Jupiter. Behind the old man, on the black rock, stand the Sun and Moon.

---

## CHAPTER THE FIFTH.

### *Of the Conversion of Prepared Mercury into Mercurial earth.*

Metals, as above stated, contain a salt, out of which fire and the sagacity of the artist can educe a water, which the Sages call Mercurial water, the Virgin's milk, Lunaria, May dew, the Green Lion, the Dragon, the Fire of the Sages. This Mercurial water they

have compared to corrosive aqua fortis,
because just as those waters which are
composed out of atrament, alum, cop-
peras, Armenian salt, etc., corrode
metals, and break them up, so this
Mercurial spirit, or water, dissolves
its body, and separates from it the
Tincture.

The picture represents a hill, on
which stand many trees ; at the foot of
the hill is a yellow lion suckling a green
lion.

There is a furnace in which is a
pumpkin-shaped vessel (cucurbit), from

which blue serpents ascend into the alembic, and are collected into a receptacle by an old man who seems on the point of carrying it away.

———

## CHAPTER THE SIXTH.

### *Of the Exaltation of Mercurial Water.*

The ancient Sages have spoken of the composition of the Green Lion or Dragon, emanating from the seven Planets, in a style saturated with the darkness of night itself; but instead of vainly endeavouring to untie their Gordian knots, I will try to sketch its composition with a few strokes of my pen. It is generated by the subtle influences descending into the elements; then its substance is scattered abroad in the heavens, its workshop is in the clouds, and again it descends into its earth, with rain water and a white vapour, thus receiving the strength of things above and things below; it is nourished by its own body, eating its

wings and tail with its teeth, the whole
body being swallowed by the head, and
remaining in it for ever. This is the
hidden and incomparable treasure of all
the Sages, which none can obtain except through the teaching of a Master,
or by revelation of God, who, in His
goodness makes it known to whom He
will.

An old man stands near a vessel,
like an urinal, in which a Green Dragon
is devouring blue serpents.  Above the
Dragon is the yellow, green, blue, black,
red sign of Mercury.  Above the urinal is
a Green Dragon biting its tail.  Near

the urinal a Green Lion bites a piece
out of the back of a Red Lion, so that
the blood flows down. In the back-
ground are forests and hills.

---

## CHAPTER THE SEVENTH.

### *Of the Solution of the Sun with Mercurial Water.*

It should be noted at this point
that the Tincture is not found otherwise
than in gold. This may be understood
from the parable of Bernard, who says
that the Sun, on entering the bath, first
of all puts off his golden robe. For
what the eagle is among birds, the lion
among beasts, the salmon among fishes,
the Sun among planets, such gold is
among metals  In it are the red and
white tincture, because it tinges, transforms, and illumines all bodies. For
gold is made out of the substance of the
most subtle living Mercury, and out of
pure, red, fixed, self-cleansed Sulphur,
which tinges, and contains in itself, the
soul, which is called the form of gold,

and by some Sages the Ferment of
Philosophers. This soul of gold with
its heat digests and tinges its substance,
and imparts to it its form, so that
through its mediation the day begins to
dawn. To corrupt the gold, to dissolve
and volatilize it while still preserving its
form, is our great object, as it is also
our grand labour.

The Sun, encircled by a red rainbow, shines among the clouds, and a
Green Lion is biting the Sun in the face,
so that the blood flows. An old man is
holding in his hand an urinal, in which

is red water; and in this water a winged man stands up to his navel. Out of the urinal is flying a Green Dragon, which bites the face of the Sun as he stands with the Moon on a rock, so that the blood flows under the dragon into the urinal. Under the black rock is a Green Dragon, whose tail is cut off, and the same is gnawing his wings.

---

## CHAPTER THE EIGHTH.

### *Of the Preparation of the Earth, or Moon of the Sages.*

When the soul of gold has been separated from its body, or when the body, in other words, has been dissolved, the body of the Moon should be watered with its proper menstruum, and reverberated, the operation being repeated as often as necessary, *i.e.*, until the body becomes subtle, broken up, pure, dissolved, coagulated. This is done, not with common fire, but with that of the Sages, and at last you must see clearly that nothing remains undis-

solved. For unless the Moon or Earth
is properly prepared and entirely emptied
of its soul, it will not be fit to receive
the Solar Seed; but the more thoroughly the earth is cleansed of its impurity and earthiness, the more vigorous
it will be in the fixation of its ferment.
This earth or Moon of the Sages is the
trunk upon which the solar branch of
the Sages is engrafted. This earth,
with its water, putrefies and is cleansed;
for heat, acting on a dry substance,
causes whiteness. Azot and fire wash
Laton, or earth, and remove its opa-
city.

A fire is laid under the Sun, which is burning, and much smoke is ascending. An old man has in his hands an urinal, in which is the Moon lying on her back in blackish water. Out of the vessel is flying a green Dragon, holding the Moon in its mouth by the navel, and placing its fore feet on a black rock. Beneath the rock a green Dragon lies dead on his back.

---

## CHAPTER THE NINTH.

### *The Conjunction of Sun and Moon.*

The ancient philosophers have enumerated several kinds of conjunction, but to avoid a vain prolixity I will affirm, upon the testimony of Marsilius Ficinus, that conjunction is union of separate qualities or an equation of principles, viz., Mercury and Sulphur, Sun and Moon, agent and patient, matter and form. When the virgin, or feminine, earth is thoroughly purified and purged from all superfluity, you must give it a husband meet for it; for

when the male and the female are joined
together by means of the sperm, a generation must take place in the menstruum.  The substance of Mercury is
known to the Sages as the earth and
matter in which the Sulphur of Nature
is sown, that it may there putrefy, the
earth being its womb.   Here the female
seed awaits that of the male, by means
of which they are inseparably united,
the one being hot and dry, and the
other cold and moist; the heat and dryness of the male are tempered with the
cold and moisture of the female, and, in
due time, the matter will assume a
specific form.  For all action tends to
the production of a form, being, as it is,
an efficient principle.

### OPPOSITION.

A very red Sun is pouring blood
into an urinal.  An old man is pouring
blood out of another urinal, together
with a winged child, into a third urinal,
which stands on straw and contains
the Moon lying on her back in blackish

water. Near the Sun a jug is pouring white rays, or drops, into an urinal. On the hill stands a Phœnix, biting its

breast, out of which drops blood, the same being drunk by its young. Beneath the rock a husbandman is scattering seed in his field.

---

### CHAPTER THE TENTH.

*Of the Blackness or Raven's Head by means of which the copulation of Sun and Moon takes place* ...

The second conjunction is of three, viz., body, soul, and spirit; and these three we must make one. For as the soul is the bond of the spirit, so the body must also join to itself the soul, which can only be after putrefaction; for nothing can be improved if its form has not previously been utterly destroyed. The signs of this are a black colour and a fetid smell. For heat, acting on moisture, produces blackness, which is the sign of the perfect mingling of the substance with a specific form. For solution and putrefaction begin with a fetid smell, and the process gradually develops, and therefore the Raven's Head is called a deadly poison. The odour is rather intellectually than sensuously perceptible. The blackness must precede whiteness. For putrefaction begins with solution, but does not end with it. The second solution of the more perfect stone is better than the first, because the more it develops, the more the stone is subtilized. Our whole magistery, then, is based on putrefaction; for it can come to nothing, unless it is putrefied.

CONJUNCTION.

BLACK SUN       BLACK MOON.

An old man with a book in his hand
stands by the furnace.

A black Sun in the vessel.

Behind the furnace is a field of green
barley springing up out of the earth.

The Pavement, on which the furnace
stands, is black.

---

CHAPTER THE ELEVENTH.

*Of the Peacock's Tail.*

Our substance, according to the
Sages, has a red head, white feet, and

black eyes.   The beginning of our work is the Black Raven, which, like all things that are to grow and receive life, must first putrefy.   For putrefaction is a necessary condition of solution, as solution is of birth and regeneration. This putrefaction is not impure, but a commixtion, in their smallest parts, of earth with water, and water with earth, till the whole body becomes one.   The red male must be digested in union with his white wife, till both become dry— for otherwise no colours will appear. When the dry principle acts on the moist, flowers of all the colours of a Peacock's Tail begin to spring up in the Sage's vessel.   Sometimes the vessel will seem inwardly covered with gold, which is a sign of the action of the male seed, or Sulphur, on the female menstruum, or Mercury, one mingling with the other as the result of their con- flict.   As the moisture is gradually dried up, these shifting colours give place to a settled whiteness.

An old man stands near the furnace, both towers are open, the urinal con-

stantly changes its colour; behind the furnace is barley producing ears.

---

## Chapter the Twelfth.

### *Of the White Tincture.*

Having treated of the matter, the mode of procedure, and of the regimen of the fire, I proceed now to the description of the composition of the white and the red Stone. The blackness becomes whiteness very slowly; the operation must be gradual, as a fierce fire would burst the vessel, and mar our work. As the Mercury becomes white, our white Sulphur becomes incombustible, containing the poison, whose whiteness is like the whiteness of alabaster. The whole magistery takes place in one vessel, and with one fire, viz., the dry and moist elementary fire of the matter, till it is all dissolved again and again, and coagulated and thickened into a mass of a clear snow-white colour, which, when cool, becomes like a hard gum. The decoction, however, must be continued till the Eagle is revived (or vitrified), and becomes a crystalline stone which melts, tinges, and coagulates Mercury and other imperfect metals into pure silver. This white tincture, or elixir, is also called the Virgin's milk, the everlasting water, and water of life, because it is as brilliant as white marble; it is also called the White Queen, who by increasing the fire becomes the Mighty King, the white transforming into yellow and saffron, and at last into a deep ruby colour.

A white King sits on the throne, having at his feet the Moon, and the five Planets on their knees. Near at hand

is a field, with yellow, ripening ears of barley. Behind the furnace is an old man inspecting the coals, and in the urinal is the full Moon.

———

CHAPTER THE THIRTEENTH.

*Of the Perfect Red Elixir.*

Xiphilinus and the rest of the philosophers agree in this, that the white colour must precede the red. As

you can have no red colour where the
substance has not first been white, so
the black cannot become orange unless
it first become white. In like manner,
the Rosary says that nothing can become gold that has not first been silver.
He who knows how to convert gold into
silver, also knows how to convert silver
into gold. Gold, to become silver, must
first be corrupted and made black, and
there is no method of becoming yellow
except by way of white; in the same
way the white must become red by way
of yellow. Heat, acting on moisture,
causes blackness; acting on dryness.
especially if it be continued carefully and
unceasingly, there is developed true
whiteness; out of white comes yellow,
and out of yellow a permanent and
tinging ruby colour.

An old man in a tunic stands by a furnace, one tower of which is open, and in the urinal of the other is a purple Sun.

A King, like a Pontiff, in a
purple robe, sits on the throne, and at
his feet kneel the Sun and Moon, with
the five planets ; behind the King stands
an old man with uncovered head.

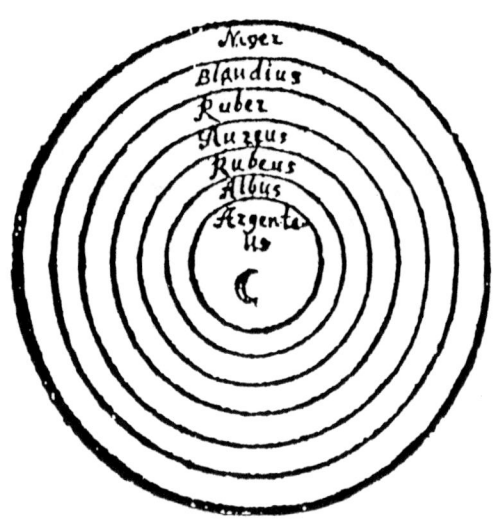

The Circles are : 1, Black ; 2, Blue ;
3, Red ; 4, Golden; 5, Ruddy ; 6,White ;
7, Argentine, with the sign of the Moon.

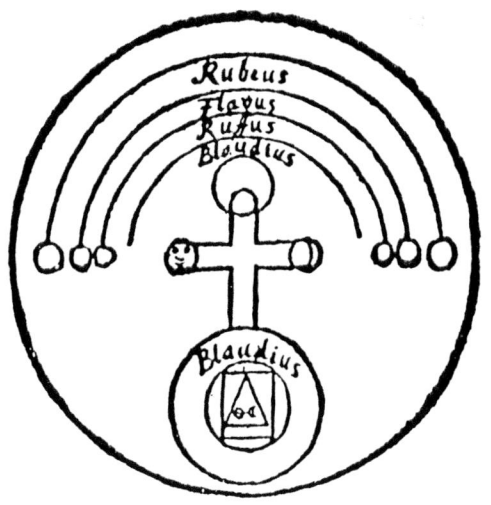

The Circle is black, white, blue, red, yellow, tawny, blue; in the Cross are the Sun and Moon. The lower Circle is blue, and contains a quadrangle of red, blue, black, and white. The triangle is black, blue, and red, and in its centre are the Sun and Moon.

END.

# INDEX.

---